Brittenden Leeds

THE TRANSFORMING FRIENDSHIP

A Book About Jesus and Ourselves

By
LESLIE D. WEATHERHEAD
M.A., F.R.G.S., HON. C.F.

Author of
'After Death,' 'The Mystery of Pain,'
'The After World of the Poets,'
'Psychology in Service of the Soul,'
'The Mastery of Sex,'
'Jesus and Ourselves,'
'Coming to Christ in Modern Days,'
'The Old Testament and To-day' (*jointly*), &c.

LONDON
THE EPWORTH PRESS
(EDGAR C. BARTON)
25-35 CITY ROAD, E.C.1

First Edition . . .	*February* 1928
Second Edition . .	*October* 1928
Third Edition . . .	*December* 1928
Fourth Edition . . .	*May* 1929
Fifth Edition . . .	*November* 1929
Sixth Edition . . .	*February* 1930
Seventh Edition . . .	*May* 1930
Eighth Edition . .	*October* 1930
Ninth Edition . . .	*January* 1931
Tenth Edition	*July* 1931
Eleventh Edition . .	*October* 1931
Twelfth Edition . .	*February* 1932
Thirteenth Edition . . .	*May* 1932
Fourteenth Edition . .	*November* 1932
Fifteenth Edition . .	*February* 1933
Sixteenth Edition . .	*September* 1933
Seventeenth Edition . .	*February* 1934
Eighteenth Edition . . .	*May* 1934
Nineteenth Edition . .	*December* 1934
Twentieth Edition . .	*August* 1935
Twenty-first Edition .	*January* 1936
Twenty-second Edition .	*September* 1936

Made and Printed in Great Britain by
The Camelot Press Limited,
London and Southampton

To

LYN

TRUE WIFE AND TRUEST FRIEND

WHO HAS TAUGHT ME SO MUCH CONCERNING
HUMAN FRIENDSHIP
AS TO DEEPEN MY FAITH IN THAT WHICH
IS DIVINE

PREFACE

THE substance of the following pages has been preached to my congregation at Brunswick Wesleyan Church, Leeds, to the members of which it is the greatest joy and privilege of my life to minister, not only in the pulpit and in the home, but in a certain private room at the church, which, to many, as to the writer, has become a sacred place, since, within its walls, the discovery has been made and re-made which is expressed in the line,

> Thy touch has still its ancient power.

Most of these chapters, though they have all been re-written, appeared first as articles in the *Methodist Recorder*, and the kind permission of the Editor to reprint them is gratefully acknowledged.

This little book is sent out into a world full of books not because the writer imagines that the thought in it is distinctive or new. If to any reader it meant that life took on a new meaning, a new purpose, or a new beauty, then the writer would feel that the publication had been justified and his own purposes achieved.

Thanks are here accorded to my father-in-law, the Rev. Arthur Triggs, and to my friend, Miss Nancy Stephenson. They have both helped me tremendously in the preparation of the book. Nor can I forbear to say here that I owe to the Rev. Dr. W. R. Maltby—to what he has said in conversations and addresses, and to what he is—almost all that is of value in my own thought and experience, though of course the writer alone must be held responsible for the views expressed.

L. D. W.

LEEDS.

NOTE.

Special permission has been received for the quotations referred to below. Where necessary the fees have been paid. The author desires to express his gratitude to the following:

Messrs. Burns Oates & Washbourne Ltd., for quotations from Francis Thompson.

Messrs. Chatto & Windus and Messrs. A. P. Watt & Son for quotation from George Macdonald.

The Editor of the *Spectator* for quotation from Wilfred Brinton.

Messrs. Smith, Elder & Co., for quotations from Robert Browning.

Messrs. Macmillan & Co. Ltd., for quotation from Sir Rabindranath Tagore.

Messrs. Charles Scribner's Sons for quotation from Sydney Lanier.

Mrs. Katherine Tynan Hickson and Messrs. Sidgwick & Jackson for quotation from Katherine Tynan.

Mr. Rudyard Kipling and to Messrs. Methuen & Co., Ltd., for quotation from Rudyard Kipling.

CONTENTS

PROLOGUE

A MODERN VISION OF JESUS

But (when so sad thou canst not sadder)
Cry ;—and upon thy so sore loss
Shall shine the traffic of Jacob's ladder
Pitched betwixt Heaven and Charing Cross.

Yea, in the night, my Soul, my daughter,
Cry,—clinging Heaven by the hems ;
And lo, Christ walking on the water
Not of Gennesareth, but Thames !

FRANCIS THOMPSON.

PROLOGUE

A MODERN VISION OF JESUS

WHAT we need as we embark on this quest of Christ is to get a picture of Him clearly in our minds. Not a picture which is that of the ecclesiastical and conventional stained-glass window. Not a picture thrown on to the screen of the mind by the language of creeds and confessions of faith. Not even the picture painted by the gospel writers in a setting two thousand years old. Rather, the glorious Figure of the gospel picture in a modern setting. Not Jesus standing with arms outstretched, a sunset sky behind Him, while in the quiet Sabbath evening light a number of supplicants, picturesquely dressed, bow before Him. Aestheticism may conceal reality and become an orgy of sensuousness. Rather, Jesus among the kind of people we know; Jesus among the kind of people we are. Can we recover the atmosphere, the spirit of Jesus' attitude to men and women like ourselves?

Imagine Him, then, in modern life. It has been truly said that Jesus could go into any Army mess, into any factory dining-hall, into any business or professional common-room, into any hotel or boarding-house, into any students' hostel or college, and His presence would not make men uncomfortable. His second visit would be eagerly looked for.

Why? Rarely did condemnation pass those gentle lips (unless men were religious hypocrites or cruel to little children); but in His presence men felt their inner, better selves suddenly revived within them. Jesus lifted up men's hearts. He saw all their dormant possibilities. What is more, He made men see them, and, what is more still, He made men desire, with a deep and passionate longing, that those possibilities should actualize, and His dreams for them come true; He made men believe that they *could* come true. His utter sincerity made men see their own insincerity, and instinctively turn from it with loathing and contempt. He made men want to be like Him; and when He talked with them, men felt that likeness to Him had suddenly become possible, and that life would never be true or beautiful till they set this goal definitely before them.

So there is in the world to-day that same insistent—though sometimes inarticulate—cry: 'Sir, we would see Jesus.' He must shine again in all His winsome loveliness, not remote, but near; the ever available,

Not of Gennesareth, but Thames!

Jesus has only to be truly seen to be loved, and when we love we shall be prepared to follow. An effort will be made to convey the desired impression by four visions or dreams.

. . . .

I saw in my dream that Jesus came to a great city and stayed in the house of a certain business man. And one morning, the man, thinking to please his Guest, said, 'I will show you the church where I worship.' But Jesus said, 'No; show me the business where you work.' So the man took Jesus and showed Him round his business, and Jesus took an interest in all He saw. But He was not allowed to see everything. He did not see rooms where men worked like rats in dark and dirty holes. Other things also the man concealed; but Jesus did not say anything. And in my dream I could not tell whether He knew that He was being deceived. Taking Him into a private office the man showed Jesus his books and his last balance sheet. Jesus sat in the office chair, and, His finger on the page, read through every item. At some items He paused, and, though He did not say a word, the man's face was covered with blushes and his heart throbbed with shame, for he could see that Jesus knew all that had happened before some items could be entered into the credit side. Then, very quietly, Jesus spoke. 'I will write the true balance sheet,' He said. I could not see all that He wrote, but on the debit side were entries like this: 'Men kept overtime so late that they were utterly fatigued, their spirits depressed, and temptation found them spent and exhausted'; 'The wrong man made foreman in the workshop; a shrewd man but a bully; the lives of many embittered, the lives of some made fearful'; 'Practices continued after the discovery that they were wrong.' And on the credit side were entries such as these: 'An interest in the personal happiness of certain men'; 'The refusal to do a big stroke of business by an underhand method'; 'A little trouble to see that really good work was turned out.'

And when Jesus had finished writing, I could see that there was something the man wanted to say, and at last, after much hesitation, he said it. 'Business is business,' he murmured; 'everybody does these things. If I don't do them my business will suffer, and with me my wife and children.' And Jesus looked into the man's eyes as though He perfectly understood, and, indeed, sympathized. But He said, 'Don't lose your life in trying to find it.' And there were tears in the man's eyes.

And the man took Jesus and showed Him all the things which previously he had concealed. But Jesus never said a word of condemnation. He just said, 'You will be far happier when you have altered it all. Don't be afraid. Your heavenly Father knows what you need.'

And in my dream I was allowed to look into the future, and I saw that the man became much poorer, and many said he was a fool. But there was peace in his heart, and a shining gladness in his eyes, and not a trace of worry in his soul. And I wondered in my dream whether he would become rich; but I learned that the man himself did not even care.

And so my dream of Jesus and the business man ended.

And in my second dream I saw Jesus in the home. It was not clear in the dream whether it was a rich or a poor home. It seemed to me that Jesus would be the same in any home. From the moment that He entered it with His 'Peace be to this house,' the little children were captivated by Him. I had sometimes imagined that He would only be merry in a dignified and reserved kind of way. But He played with the children with absolute abandon. He got down on His hands and knees, and the little ones climbed up on His back. He was full of fun and brimful of happiness. He was like a child Himself. And when it was time for them to go to bed, He carried the tiny ones up Himself and tucked them in, and heard them say their little prayers.

After they had gone to bed Jesus stayed and talked with their mother. And in my dream I could see behind her mind, and I knew that she was seeking the help of Jesus. That is one of the strange things about Jesus. People always feel they want to tell Him all their difficulties and get His help.

So the mother poured out her troubles, her problems, her grief. Jesus never interrupted her once. And He seemed to understand so perfectly that in His very listening there was a strange comfort. It was a long list of worries: the drudgery of housework, the servant problem, the meals, the demands of society inside and outside the house, the difficulty of making ends meet, the worry about the children, the wondering what they should become, the lack of time to teach them as she would like. And I wondered what Jesus would say.

He asked a lot of questions, especially about the parents' own ideals in the home; what did they want the home to stand for? what were their ideals for their children? And the mother told Him her *ideals*; but she found that always between ideal and its realization seemed to come some barrier or other. I remember wondering in my dream if Jesus would reproduce some of His own recorded teaching; or whether He would tell her to get away and have a holiday. But He just looked into her face with a quiet, loving look, until it seemed as if some strange wave of helpfulness emanated from Him. And very quietly He spoke to her about an inward peace. He had nothing to say about the servant problem. He hurled no reproaches against modern society. He just said that nothing mattered so much as that inward peace which all could possess, and which He Himself so evidently had. All other concerns not only sunk into insignificance before it, *they were solved in it*. 'We are all in the Father's hands,' He said, in His quiet voice, 'and in quiet, waiting trustfulness, there will come the grace we need.'

And in my dream I was allowed to see into the future, and I saw that all the problems of that house had been solved since the coming of Jesus. There was no lessening of the gaiety and fun, but a certain irritability, that I had noticed before, had vanished, and there was a great calm. The home was like a lovely garden, and the little child-flowers were neither forced in a moral hot-house nor left to struggle in the gloom. They just grew up in the sunshine.

And so my dream about Jesus in the home ended.

In my third dream I saw a young man who was

a university student. He was seated alone in his own small room, with his books on the table before him. He was of magnificent physique, but he was very lonely and his heart was disconsolate. There was almost a haunted look on his face. And as I looked into his mind I saw that it was in a state of war. The good was fighting the evil, and the issue was still uncertain. His room was a symbol of the state of his mind. The walls were covered with vulgar pictures cut from cheap magazines. And yet, on a little shelf away in a corner, was a photograph of his mother.

I do not remember that I heard the door open, in my dream. I became aware that Jesus was sitting opposite the student in the bare little room. The knowledge came to me as one becomes aware of the light of some lovely dawn amid the baleful glittering lights of some belated orgy. 'You thought of Me,' said the quiet voice which I had learned in my dreams to love, 'and so I am here.'

I knew also that Jesus could see the battle that was raging in the young man's mind. I knew that the fiery temptations of youth, the rash impetuousness, the desire to 'see life,' were battling with an ideal of a clean, manly life. And the look in Jesus' face made me think of those words, 'Jesus looking upon him, loved him.'

Then there came to me a strange impression. It seemed as though there emanated from Jesus a spirit of belief in the possibilities of the man before Him. And he held up his head at once. Indeed, any man may well hold up his head if Jesus believes in him. And, although no question had been asked, the student said very quietly, ' I will begin again.' And Jesus smiled.

That is another strange thing about Jesus. He has the power to see below the surface into the very depths of the heart. He sees the seeds of lovely flowers where others see only the ugly brown soil that hides them. It is not so true to say that He loves the unlovable as to say that in every one He sees something lovable. And, when the student saw that Jesus believed in him, he believed in himself, and goodness sprang into quickened growth.

Feeling that Jesus was near as never before, there flashed into the student's mind an impetuous wish to ask Him about some of the intellectual religious difficulties that were troubling him. And Jesus, reading his thoughts, said, ' Have you not seen enough ? ' And with a great light on his face the student said, ' Yes, it is enough.' He felt that he wanted no proof. The questions of Jesus' birth and the manner of His resurrection seemed remote and irrelevant. The student felt quite sure of Jesus. And, indeed, Jesus needs no credentials except Himself.

And again in my dream I was allowed to look into the future, and I saw the student in the same room, but all the vulgar pictures had been taken down. I remember noticing too that the sunlight was pouring in at the window. And when I looked into his mind I saw that there, too, many thought-pictures had disappeared ; that there too the sun was shining.

And so my dream of Jesus and the student ended.

I dreamed again. A girl was living in a small boarding-house in the city. It was not a pleasant life. For one thing it was very, very lonely. For another it was very monotonous. She rose early in the morning, had a frugal breakfast, went to a workroom over a large shop all day, and in the evening returned to her lonely room. She had very few friends, and she was no longer very young. The other people, both in the boarding-house and in the workroom, were uncongenial.

There were occasions when life seemed just meaningless ; after the evening meal, for instance, when it was too early to go to bed, and yet there seemed nothing to do. Many and many a time she had changed her clothes—putting on the gayest things she had in an effort to make herself feel gay —and wandered out alone. But beneath the pathetic brightness of her clothing a sad heart ached dismally. She had no money to spare for amusements, and sometimes, when foul men had spoken to her, there had come even the temptation to lose all restraint and embark on a nameless life. When she had left home, life had been filled with high and beautiful ideals, but they had been lost and smothered in the dust of the actual. She had become flippant, superficial, hollow. The deep voices of the soul had been all but stifled. Life had become vulgar and mean and petty.

And yet not wholly so. For in my dream I saw

her sitting in her little room with her elbows on the hard dressing-table, her head buried in her hands, and her shoulders shaking with sobs. And, when she looked up again, her face all stained with tears, Jesus was standing by her side.

At first she stared at Him as though He were a ghost; but soon the quiet voice put her at her ease in a way she only half understood. 'Would you like to tell me all about it?' He said. There flashed through the girl's mind the thought that she would tell Him all about it, that she would pour out her complaints against others—how badly they treated her in the boarding-house; how they snubbed her in the room at business where she ate her lunch; how her superiors treated her as a machine; how lonely she was; how miserable!

And yet, when she looked into the eyes of Jesus, she felt somehow that He knew all that already, aye, and more; she felt that He knew what she never intended to tell any one—her secret temptations, and all the blank sorrow of her selfish, vain little life. But the look in Jesus' face did not frighten her. It seemed the only thing that had given her hope in herself for many a weary month. 'Tell me,' she said at last, 'what it is you see?' Very tenderly came His answer: 'I see the possibilities of a glorious womanhood. I see the possibilities of a life dedicated to God.' 'Do you see nothing else?' she questioned; 'nothing of sordidness, of greed, of vanity; of something—something baser even than that?' 'I see,' He answered, 'far below that, a deep desire for purity, and a hatred of all that is unbeautiful in life.' 'But,' she said, 'I have broken all my resolutions. I have lost my chances. I have lost my ideals. I have lost my faith.' Quietly came the sound of the Beloved Voice, but with a ring of deep assurance: 'The Son of Man came to seek and to save that which was lost.'

It seemed to the girl that He had given her back her youth. For now life seemed suddenly filled with a new and glorious and indomitable hope. It was springtime in her soul. Life had become beautiful and infinitely desirable. Life could *never* be the same again. Her better self had risen, phoenix-like, above the ashes of the girl who was dead.

And Jesus looked at her with a smile of amazing tenderness. I could not hear, in my dream, all that He said, but as He moved towards the door I heard Him say, 'And you will never be alone again; every day I am with you.' She held the door for Him, and lingered a moment, half hoping that He would speak again or turn round. But He passed out in silence and was gone. Then, very softly, she closed the door.

I

THE GIFT OF THE FRIENDSHIP

If for all your evil you know how to give your children what is good, how much more will your Father give the holy Spirit from Heaven to those who ask Him ? (Moffatt).

Luke xi. 13.

If thou knewest the gift of God . . .

John iv. 10.

Repent, and be baptized, every one of you in the name of Jesus Christ for the remission of sins ; and ye shall receive the gift of the Holy Ghost.

Acts ii. 38.

On the Gentiles also was poured out the gift of the Holy Ghost.

Acts x. 45.

God gave them the like gift as He did unto us.

Acts xi. 17.

The gift, by grace, which is by one man, Jesus Christ, hath abounded unto many.

Rom. v. 15.

God's free gift is the Life of the Ages bestowed upon us in Christ Jesus our Lord (Weymouth).

Acts vi. 23.

Thanks be unto God for His unspeakable gift.

2 Cor. ix. 15.

Each one of us is granted his own grace, as determined by the full measure of Christ's gift (Moffatt).

Eph. iv. 7.

I

THE GIFT OF THE FRIENDSHIP

CHRISTIANITY must seem to some people a very complex and difficult thing. Sermons are preached on it, books are written about it, conferences are held to discuss it, a single word in the Gospels frequently takes a commentator several pages of a big book to explain. Yet surely the essence of the Christian message must be very simple. The people who took it from Jesus' lips were not clever people. They were very hungry people. That was their main qualification.

I think the essence of the matter might be stated by saying that Christianity is the acceptance of the gift of the friendship of Jesus. I asked a number of intimate friends recently where they would *begin* with a man who was penitent about the past, who really wanted to have done with it, who really wanted to find the new life about which the New Testament writers knew so much and we so little. One man said he would have to know the circumstances of the man's 'case' first. That seemed to me an evasion. Another said he would instruct the man to go home, and pray and read the Bible. That doesn't sound very exciting. Another said it was quite simply stated—'Believe on the Lord Jesus Christ and thou shalt be saved.' That doesn't sound very explicit. One said that it was a matter of imitating Christ. It sounds a hopeless business. Another, who has been preaching for forty years, said it was a matter of the will. That doesn't seem much of a gospel. Another man said that he had found that the first thing to do was to straighten out intellectual difficulties.

I am quite sure they were all right as far as secondary things went. At least, there was a bit of truth in it all. I think they were all wrong about the *beginning* of the matter. Then I asked a layman, white-haired, and, as I once thought, narrow-minded. He took up his Bible. I can hear his quiet voice now. . . . 'How much more shall your heavenly Father give the Holy Spirit to them that ask Him.' He said that the new life was a gift from God. You simply had to kneel down and ask for it, and then get up and believe that you had received it, go out and live as if you had received it, only to find that it was yours indeed. That layman helped me enormously, because from all the tangle of thought he took me right back to the beginning. I found about fifty passages scattered all over the New Testament in which the New Life is spoken of as a gift. I think that is the beginning of the good news. God gives me a gift.

How can I take this gift? After all, when Jesus lived in Galilee, His friendship was an easy thing to take. He was so obviously there, and His friendliness expressed itself in deeds that all men might see, in words that all men might hear. It sounds such an easy thing to say that one may accept the gift, but to some practical minds it almost seems like self-deception. Let us think how a little child accepts the friendship of Jesus. When she kneels to say her evening prayer she *imagines* that some one is there ; tall and dark, in a white robe, with a very kind face, and perhaps a hand stretched out on her head. She is taking hold of the gift of His friendship by the faculty of her imagination. Of course, one might say at once that in the same way she may imagine fairies, but as she grows older, her experience will give the lie to the existence of fairies, but her experience, if allowed to develop naturally, will never deny the friendship of Jesus. All the history of the Church and the lives of all the saints vouch for this tremendous reality. Nor, we think, is there any other way in which the gift of this friendship can be appropriated, and one feels that the imaginative faculty can have no higher exercise than this. One would dare to say to a person, 'Imagine He walks by your side. If you can bear the word, *pretend* that it is true ; and then you will find in your own experience how true it is, and imagination will grow up into faith.' After all, faith is imagination grown up.

One ought not to suggest that there will be anything uncanny in one's experience of His presence, for reasons which we shall see later. One should not look for vision, or listen for voice, yet the sense of presence will become overwhelmingly real, and leave no doubt as to its validity. It cannot be realized by intellectual keenness, nor by effort of will, but by appropriation through that imaginative faculty on which depends all real faith.

I have come home from some meetings thoroughly tired and disappointed and disillusioned. I have settled down in an arm-chair with bitterness in my veins instead of blood. There was a desire to write a letter calculated to crush one's opponent, and phrases which would silence him thronged on to the threshold of the mind. I was too tired to pray, too tired to stir up any desire to pray, and then I tried an experiment. I relaxed the body and relaxed the mind, left, as it were, the door of the mind ajar. There was very little more than a vague longing for the coming of the Friend, that Friend who understands, who understands our worst moments without losing belief in our best. And then something happened. The peace which is indescribable flooded the whole spirit; a hush which is ineffable quieted the mind. I have never seen a vision, I have never heard a voice, but I have felt that the last thing I wanted to do was to write the letter, and the last words I wanted to use were those which would have brought the pride of an opponent down to the dust. And there is only one explanation of such an experience. God's greatest gift to men was given and accepted. The Friend *came*.

So God gives us a gift for which we need not strive, and about which primarily we need not argue. After all, our attitude to a gift is acceptance. This sounds profound, but is certainly true, especially of any one with Scotch blood in his veins. If a man offers me a thousand pounds I do not knock him down, I do not have to struggle to get it. I take it and go home before he changes his mind. Nor do I say to him, 'I am sorry, but I can't take it until I can understand the intellectual basis on which it is being given.' I put it in the bank and am content to leave the intellectual basis until the next morning. I may never see the actual money; it may be paid into my bank; but if I trust the donor I go and draw cheques on it and find them honoured. The central experience of the Christian life is a gift which I cannot see, but which is certainly there, and mine, for I draw cheques to any amount on it and find them honoured of God every day. Let us examine more fully some of the false emphases we commonly make.

First, the false emphasis on struggle. To how many people is that the main note in their Christian life! A note of battle. There is a place for the use of the will, of course, but there is no good news in telling a man that his will is all that counts; that he must 'try harder.' People are tired of trying. The preacher who urges them along the jaded ways of the harassed will is putting new burdens on, instead of taking burdens off. People pathetically try to respond. Every communion service, every watch-night, every birthday some of us make new resolutions to try again. Again and again God makes a silence in our lives. We listen to the birds at dawn, or the moan of the sea at night. We gaze into the heart of a flower, or watch the flaming sky at sunset. We spend an hour under the quiet stars. The hush of the Infinite is upon us. We tell ourselves we will try again. God sends love into our life, and we stand with the beloved at His altar. And we tell ourselves we will try again. Comes a day when we hold our first-born in our arms; that bit of our two selves and God. And we say, 'I will be a better man now.' Comes a day when the blinds are drawn, and voices are hushed, and all the house is still. We stand by a grave as deep as life, as long as love, and as wide as desire, and then turn away saying to ourselves, 'I will try to be a better man.' And our sins mock us openly. We try and try and try, and nearly break under the strain. Religion is increasingly a burden, when it ought to be, in Samuel Rutherford's phrase, 'the kind of burden sails are to a ship, wings are to a bird.' People are pushing a religion when it ought to be carrying them; which is just as silly as a man who pushes his motor-bike ten miles because he will not accept the *gift* of a tin of petrol from a friend. There is something that fires the will. It is the acceptance by faith of a new life which is God's gift to any who will take. That is worth calling good news. If God were unwilling to give this gift, all our striving would not make Him give it. And if He is willing to give it, there is nothing to strive for or against, except our own doubts that the gift is ours for the asking. So Paul, even to his down-and-outs, does not say, 'Try harder.' He says, 'Believe differently'—which is a gospel. And when he tells men to fight, it is a fight of *faith* to which they are urged. The only battle is a battle with our doubts. 'Not by might and not by power, but by My Spirit, saith the Lord.'

There is also a false emphasis on intellectual belief. It is very important that we should have our believing right. We need an intelligent theology which, while it transcends reason, does not at any point contradict it. Yet the need for straightening out our theology is nowhere near the *beginning* of the gospel of Jesus Christ. Jesus did not demand intellectual assent to a creed. He did not question Peter as to whether he was sound on the inspiration of the Old Testament. He said, 'Follow Me.' Peter accepted the gift of a transforming friendship with Jesus. Then he made his own theology afterwards out of his own experience. And that is the only kind of creed which can be of any use to any of us. Not the creed that I take over from my great-grandfather and try to press into my experience. That is an extra burden to be carried. But the creed that is born in the silent places of my spirit out of my own experience of a gift given to me—that is not a burden I have to carry, but a pair of wings which will carry me. You cannot catch a motor-bus in a crinoline. You have to wear clothes which meet the spirit and demand of the time. You cannot make a religion of any value by taking over the intellectual clothes of ages past, though they are interesting as museum specimens. You must have a working knowledge of God which is born of your own experience of Him (not some one else's), *and which is the intellectual counterpart of the new life found in Him.*

People who say they are shy of religion because of the intellectual difficulties connected with it, frequently are hiding behind a lie. The greatest religious difficulty is not intellectual, but the difficulty of being loyal to the Friend. And the loyalty doesn't break down through doubt. It breaks down through far more primitive things. It is not the Virgin Birth that troubles us. It is sensuality. It is not the doctrine of the Eternal Sonship. It is selfishness. We do not refuse other gifts simply because we do not understand them. If a man offers to fit out my home with wireless, I do not say, 'Oh, please don't, because I am not sure how it works.' Much less, if I am ill, do I object to be taken to a nursing-home in a motor-car because I do not understand the differential principle in the back axle. None of us understands *how* the gift of God makes all the difference to life. The psycho-analyst cannot tell us that. Indeed, if we had to give up either the part of religion we were able to understand or the part we were unable to understand, we had far better give up the former, since it would be much the smaller part. Some of the best men and women in the world know least of the manner of working of their religion. Imagine a theologian born before his time taking Peter on one side by the Galilean lake and explaining the Catholic Faith according to the *Quicunque Vult*; namely, 'That we worship one God in Trinity, and Trinity in Unity, neither confounding the persons nor dividing the substance. . . . The Father uncreate, the Son uncreate, the Holy Ghost uncreate. The Father incomprehensible, the Son incomprehensible, the Holy Ghost incomprehensible . . . But there are not three incomprehensible nor three uncreated, but one uncreated and one incomprehensible . . . ,' and so on for page after page till you get to this : ' He therefore that will be saved must think thus of the Trinity.' Why, long before that, Peter would have been using fishermen's language. At least he would have said, ' I go a-fishing.' And I for my part would add, ' I also go with thee.' No ! I am sure it is simpler than that ! The august truths behind that language may all be true, but God help the poor soul who *begins* there ! ' Ask and it shall be given you.' That is better. Any wayfaring man, however foolish, can take a gift. That is the beginning of the gospel.

There is also a false emphasis on imitation. I went to hear Kreisler play the violin. There were tears in my eyes in three minutes. In three minutes he took you right into the *lachrymae rerum*. He made his violin say things which are unutterable. It was like listening to the voice of humanity crying out in the wilderness of the infinite. The violin laughed and moaned and whimpered. It whispered and comforted and crooned. It sobbed and yearned and agonized. It was speaking in a language too vast and deep for human ears to understand. Tell me to imitate him ? How *can* I ? I can imitate the way he wears his hair. I can imitate his tie and his baggy trousers. But if I tried for a thousand years I could never play like that. If I practised, if I studied the instrument—no ; nothing could take me where he is. He has received a gift. If some one could implant in me Kreisler's mind and soul I might get skill by practice. Isn't that taking us nearer? You cannot imitate a living thing successfully. Imitation roses look all right to us sometimes; but they rarely deceive the bees. And people who make them never get the scent right, there is something spurious about it all. Your difficulty is that you cannot put the life force inside the rose which makes it what it is. Nor can even a living wild rose be made into a fine one by anything done externally. Not by dunging, or training, or binding. No; it must receive a gift of life from a higher type of rose, and that must be accepted in the grafting process, and then we shall have fine roses. So we may try to alter our lives by good resolutions and intentions, by imitations and effort, but how fruitless it all is until we open our lives to His friendship and are transformed like a grafted rose, not from without, but from within. It is the precious gift within that makes the difference.

So it is with all creative art. Some American tourists visited the Lake District with guide-books and a guide. With a third of their attention they listened to what the guide said, with another third they read the guide-book, and with the remaining third they had an occasional squint at the scenery. After visiting the places which Wordsworth loved so much, one of them said to the guide, 'I don't see anything very wonderful in your Lake District.' But the guide said, 'No, sir, but Wordsworth did.' He had a gift.

Thousands of us have stood by the seashore, but only Tennyson wrote,

> Break, break, break,
> On thy cold grey stones, O sea.

Thousands of us have lost our loved ones, but only Browning writes,

> O lyric Love, half angel and half bird.

You see the poet has received a gift. Put me down before an easel with all the materials an artist wants, and I can only make a daub. Turner, with the same materials, could have made something divine. He had a gift. Put me down before a piano and I can play a jig; but Paderewski, with the same number of notes, can set your soul on fire. He has a gift. God may not want to make us poets or painters or pianists, but He does want to make us saints. So He offers to *all* this gift—the gift of a new life. You can use your will-power, and that will take you part of the way. You can use your brains, and they will take you a little way. (It depends.) You can imitate, and that may take you a little way. But all these things together in music and art and poetry, and in *life*, will never take you as far as a gift will take you.

So there are a good many wearied Christians about. They are trying. So there are a good many worried Christians about. They are doing juggling tricks with their minds, and trying to bend them round impossible propositions of some one else's intellect. So there are a lot of spurious Christians about. They are imitating. Some of them are splendid people, but very, very pathetic. They do so want to be Christians. They are troubled and amazed at their failure. They are where they are because no one has ever told them where to *begin*. Many of them are looked up to as pillars of the Church. Many of them know only too well that they haven't got what the New Testament calls life at all. They are very wistful folk.

If only all three kinds of Christian would put down the noisy tools of effort, and stop arguing themselves into frenzies, and smash up their own painted mummy case, and sit down quietly, and leave the door ajar for God—Himself both Giver and Gift—then they would find that they could rise up, and do and be all that, for so long, and often with anguish and with tears, they have prayed to do and be. That is beginning at the beginning; the beginning of the gospel of Jesus Christ the Son of God. In the beginning, God.

II

THE REALITY OF THE FRIENDSHIP

O Son of Man, to right my lot,
Nought but Thy presence can avail;
Yet on the road Thy wheels are not,
Nor on the sea Thy sail!

My how, or when, Thou will not heed,
But come down Thine own secret stair,
That Thou may'st answer all my need,
Yea, every bygone prayer.

GEORGE MACDONALD.

II

THE REALITY OF THE FRIENDSHIP

Is it a real fact, practicable for everyday life in the twentieth century, that we may have communion with Jesus Christ as really as we have communion with our earthly friends? Can we know that same Jesus of Nazareth who walked about in Galilee two thousand years ago? I do not mean can we treasure His words, can we follow His way of life, can we, following His example, be heroic as He was, can we benefit by His ideas; I do not mean can we imaginatively reproduce a picture of Him clearly enough to form a substitute for His actual presence; but can we really meet Him, know Him, commune with Himself?

If so, we ought to realize what a tremendous thing this is. If all the claims of the Spiritualists were suddenly substantiated, that would be ordinary compared with this tremendous claim that Jesus is alive, and here, and apprehensible, under normal conditions, as He was in an upper room at Jerusalem so long ago. We use the language of the mystics so glibly without having passed through their experiences. Biblical passages become so familiar. Hymns have such beguiling tunes. And we soon fail to realize the tremendous things we are saying. One remembers the story of Dr. Dale at work on his book, *The Living Christ and the Four Gospels,* how he suddenly realized what had before been such a glib truth, taken for granted ; and how he walked about his study saying over and over again, ' Jesus Christ is alive, Jesus Christ is alive ! ' Drummond, in one of his books, pictures a scene which might be witnessed if Jesus actually were alive in the flesh to-day in Palestine. He pictures boats and trains loaded with pilgrims going to see Jesus. He imagines the vast crowds which would want to see Him, hear Him, touch Him, commune with Him. What if, with a little faith, we could have the central thing in that experience, and have it regularly and authentically every day of our lives ?

This great truth, which no longer startles us when it is expressed in language, and yet which is not a very common experience even now, was revolutionary enough to require a long preparation. The friendliness of God ; that was one of those priceless truths which those religious geniuses, the Jews, discovered and gave to the world, and which made a way in men's minds for the truth we are discussing now. ' Enoch walked with God.' Abraham was known as ' the friend of God.' ' God spake to Moses,' we are told, ' as a man to his friend.' David feels the valley of the shadow less dark because his Friend is with him—' Thou art with me '—and intermingled with the inspiring thoughts in the Old Testament about the majesty of God, high and lifted up, and the insignificance of man, very far below as a grasshopper, whole nations being but a drop in a bucket or the dust of a balance, is this new idea, like a friendly little river flowing through a frightening wood, of the companionship and friendliness of God.

Now look how Jesus, who always revealed His Father, who always lived to show men what God was like, consummates this idea. He did not go and live in a cave in the desert, or in some mountain fastness, to be consulted as an oracle by toiling pilgrims, who then went back without Him. He came right into the midst of man's toil. He was a toiler Himself. He was always available. He would spend all the night with a sincere seeker after truth, while an unheeding city slept. He forgot His noontide weariness if He could talk to a woman by a village well. He was never too busy or rushed or worried. He got through tremendous masses of work, and yet there was a poise of spirit, a quiet heart, an inward peace. He was 'gathered into Himself.' When you spoke to Him you never had the impression that you were intruding on the time of a very busy man. He went to each task freshly and quietly. He did that task with all the strength of His personality, and then went on to the next. And what could not be done He was quite happy to leave undone, for there were only twenty-four hours even in His day, and He gave a place of honour both to eating and sleeping. To all folk He was the same kindly, sympathetic Friend. He was never servile to the rich or condescending to the poor. Poverty nor riches, nor social position, nor education, made any difference to this Friend. 'He was a Refuge for every hunted life.' He was the personification of the friendliness of God.

And what happens when He dies? Is this fellowship broken? It is significant that Matthew represents Him as making this promise: 'Lo, I am with you all the days, even unto the consummation of the ages.' Why does He say that? In order that He may carry the friendship across the gulf of death and plant it securely on the other side, and in order that that friendship might be made available for all who needed it and had faith to make it possible.

There is nothing more beautiful in the world than the way in which Jesus established this friendship in the days between the Resurrection and the Ascension; and nowhere is His method so beautifully expounded as in Dr. Maltby's booklet, *The Meaning of the Resurrection.* Jesus will not let Mary touch Him. Why? Because He wants to take her on beyond the evidence of sight and touch. She must learn the next lesson, and realize His presence without the need of eyes and hands. He is planting the friendship in the unseen. So in the strange post-resurrection appearances. Two men, or a man and his wife perhaps, are on their way to Emmaus. Suddenly, without hearing anything, they find a Companion by their side. He walks with them, talks with them, sits with them at table. They recognize Him by the way He breaks a loaf, and then He has gone. The Twelve are gathered in the Upper Room. Suddenly they are aware of a Presence. He is there. There is a word of peace. He is gone. Again on the seashore. Again in a mountain in Galilee. Again near Bethany.

What do these strange appearings and disappearings mean? They are His perfect way of making them feel that He is never far away. He does not seem to be there. Then He breaks in upon them, always knows what has happened, always takes charge of the situation, until they never know when they may become aware of Him. They must often have turned at the opening of a door expecting to see Himself. They stopped midway in a sentence because they remembered that He could not be far away, and perhaps was an invisible auditor. The experience becomes richer. They feel that He is never absent. Communion now will mean as much as it did when they could hear His voice, see His face, and touch Him. They do not further need the offices of eye and ear and hand. He has carried the friendship beyond death; and the Ascension does not mean that He passed to some distant heaven beyond those possibilities of friendship, but that He widened the possibilities so that for all men He is the ever-available. And Pentecost was not, for them, I think, the coming of a third person, but Jesus, present in an overwhelming sense, their Friend back in their midst in power indescribable.

Whether we have realized it or not, the disciples realized it. They held no memorial service for Him. No flowers adorned His grave. No poet wrote memorial verses to Him. Unless they had been certain of His living presence and of an undying friendship which could be realized day by day, they could never have done what they did. And we are beginning to get near the answer to the question with which we started—Can the friendship of Jesus be a reality to us to-day?—when we have learned that, for a handful of very ordinary men, that friendship was the biggest reality in life, and they went to the uttermost ends of the then known world and died for the truth of that tremendous experience.

And what did that experience do for them? It did everything for them. It was the friendship that made them what they became. People who knew the disciples before they met Jesus, and who did not see them again till after the Resurrection, must have noticed a difference such as one sees in some landscape in the grip of winter, when the bitter wind howls through leafless branches, when black frost makes the ground hard and hostile to the feet, when low storm clouds make the mountains forbidding and fearful, and the moors bleak and desolate; and that same landscape when the summer sun is shining, when the trees are all in leaf, when the flowers are everywhere, and when the air is full of the sound of running brooks and the humming of bees and the singing of birds. Take Peter as such a landscape. One imagines a rough fisherman, with a ready flow of plethoric language, and a temper not easy to govern. But in all who come near Jesus manners soften, hearts become gentle. There is a new tenderness, a new sympathy, a new joy, a kind of infectious goodness. The disciples begin to say things, do things, be things, which they could never have said or done or been before. But those friends who have watched the change know the secret. 'They have been with Jesus.' The friendship has done it. Friendship will always do that for us. It will make us like the friend we admire and see much of. Merely to enter the presence of some people is to go into an atmosphere in which we become our best selves; in which nothing unworthy could be done. To live in that presence would make us new beings. To companion with Jesus must have meant a greater power to be at one's best, and a longing to do the worthy thing, and a hatred of the low, the base, and the mean.

And Christianity is meaningless unless this friendship can do as much for us. What Jesus once was, He is eternally. He comes to us, not only in His temple, or in the room when the door is shut, but as He came to Mary and Martha in the midst of household tasks, and as He came to Peter mending his nets and doing his daily work; and He comes with the same offer, the offer of His transforming friendship. There are no conditions save the imaginative faith to believe that He is, and that fellowship with Him is possible. It is an amazing offer. It means that no single experience of life has ever to be faced alone. What would it mean to us if in the temptation to hasty temper, to meanness, contempt, jealousy, impurity, avarice, we could pull ourselves up with the thought that this patient, kind, but inexorable Friend was near? What would it mean in sorrow, in bereavement, in pain, in loneliness? What would it mean in joy and laughter, in pleasure and fun? It would mean the sanctifying of every part of life. It is the experience our fathers called 'being saved,' for to be received into this friendship is to be at the end, not indeed of our journey but of all fruitless wanderings.

Can we enter into this friendship? We can. We can, as Brother Lawrence said, 'practise the Presence of God,' but the only way I know of practising the presence of God is by practising the presence of Jesus, who makes God credible and real, and entering into the transforming friendship which He offers.

Let a story told by Mr. F. W. Boreham illustrate the truth. An old Scotsman lay very ill, and his minister came to visit him. As the minister sat down on a chair near the bedside, he noticed on the other side of the bed another chair placed at such an angle as to suggest that a visitor had just left it. 'Well, Donald,' said the minister glancing at the chair, 'I see I am not your first visitor.' The Scotsman looked up in surprise, so the minister pointed to the chair. 'Ah!' said the sufferer, 'I'll tell you about the chair. Years ago I found it impossible to pray. I often fell asleep on my knees I was so tired. And if I kept awake I could not control my thoughts from wandering. One day I was so worried I spoke to my minister about it. He told me not to worry about kneeling down.

" Just sit down," he said, " and put a chair opposite you, imagine that Jesus is in it and talk to Him as you would to a friend." And,' the Scotsman added, 'I have been doing that ever since. So now you know why the chair is standing like that.' A week later the daughter of the old Scot drove up to the minister's house and knocked at his door. She was shown into the study, and when the minister came in she could hardly restrain herself. 'Father died in the night,' she sobbed. 'I had no idea death could be so near. I had just gone to lie down for an hour or two. He seemed to be sleeping so comfortably. And when I went back he was dead. He hadn't moved since I saw him before, except that *his hand was out on the empty chair at the side of the bed.* Do you understand?' 'Yes,' said the minister, 'I understand.' The Scotsman, not by intellect or will, but by an imagination which had become faith, had accepted the gift of a friendship and made the Master real. Truly 'our fellowship is with the Father and with His Son Jesus Christ.'

The reality of this transforming friendship is reached not through argument but through experience.

> The love of Jesus, what it is,
> None but His loved ones know.

But *they know.*

III

THE REALITY OF THE FRIENDSHIP TO-DAY

No fable old, no mythic lore,
  No dream of bards and seers,
No dead fact, stranded on the shore
  Of the oblivious years ;

But warm, sweet, tender, even yet
  A present help is He,
And faith has still its Olivet,
  And love its Galilee.

WHITTIER.

III

THE REALITY OF THE FRIENDSHIP TO-DAY

CHRISTIANITY began then in a vivid, tremendous, transforming experience of the friendship of Jesus. It could never have continued unless the friendship had been sustained; unless those who had never seen Him could yet enter into the fellowship and become sure of Him also. There is no greater need in our time than that those who teach religion should concern themselves, not with tightening up the machinery, developing organization, or arranging more meetings; but rather to make Jesus real to men; to invite them into that transforming fellowship which cannot be proved save by personal experience, but which, when realized, brings men that glorious exhilaration, that sense of ineffable peace, and that escape from all bondage which are promised in the New Testament.

To many, religion never has meant this, and, until it does, they will never see much in it. It is really a wonder that they are interested in it at all, for without this central experience it is little more than the beautiful thought system of a philanthropic society begun by one who, like all others, passed into the great silence never to emerge again. Our advocacy of it in their eyes must be on the same level as an invitation to join such a society, and people say, 'Don't bother me; I'm not interested. Religion is all very well in its way. I daresay it does good work. But I'm not interested. You go your way and let me go mine. You are always squabbling. You believe all sorts of fantastic things. Come down to the business of living, and you don't seem much different from anybody else.' That, roughly enough, is a diagnosis of the indifference of the multitude to religion to-day

If we could prove to them by our lives that Christianity meant first of all a transforming experience of the friendship of Jesus, an exhilaration better than wine, a joy greater than pleasure, a peace better than escape, a sense of liberty better than any free-thinker has ever enjoyed, an answer—I do not say a solution—to all life's problems, and a conquest of personal sin and depression such as the man with the strongest will in the world never dreamed could exist, then men would make a beaten track to our door, eager to know our secret, passionately, vehemently desirous to enter into it. The truth is, most of us are living on low levels of experience. We have had *some* small experience. But we are like explorers who land on some new continent, and who, on fine days and Saturday afternoons, explore some of the valleys and foothills near the coast, and then build themselves bungalows and settle down on the beach and bathe in the breakers, but who never climb the mighty mountains behind them, where the resources of a continent lie waiting to be explored. We have not realized the rich possibilities of our own faith. When we wake up to them, the world will be turned upside down again. God grant us the awakening of Mr. Kipling's 'Explorer.'

'There's no sense in going further—it's the edge of cultivation,'
So they said, and I believed it—broke my land and sowed my crop—
Built my barns and strung my fences in the little border station
Tucked away below the foothills where the trails run out and stop.

Till a voice, as bad as Conscience, rang interminable changes
On one everlasting Whisper, day and night repeated—so:
'Something hidden. Go and find it. Go and look behind the Ranges—
Something lost behind the Ranges. Lost and waiting for you. Go!' . . .

Anybody might have found it, but—His Whisper came to Me!

For some people Jesus is still imprisoned in history. They are quite sure that He was; but they do not realize that He is. They are far from realizing that most liberating truth that what He was was only the translation into terms of history of what He eternally is. To them He was the sad-eyed, dark-haired Mystic who walked in the fields and woods of Galilee, watched the waves breaking in white foam on that sunny shore, picked a few wild flowers and drew from them their story of quiet trust. He was the Dreamer of beautiful dreams such as no poets have ever seen in their hours of loftiest vision. He was the Healer who laid His hands on people's heads and cleansed them from some horrible disease; who brought forgiveness and peace to restless and sin-tortured souls. He was the Martyr, who, with thorn-crowned brow, hung from a cross upraised against a sunset sky, and who, having risen from the dead, went back to heaven and now sits on the right hand of the throne of God. It is all true. It is all very beautiful. It is inspiring. But it is a picture of the past. Its hero is a ghost flitting about the tombs of the dead years. Many people—very wistful, lovable people—when they worship, worship that picture, and in their life they try to be like its hero; and they wonder why it is so desperately difficult, why they fail so much, why they seem thrown back on themselves, why others seem to pass them with laughing, radiant faces, as if following Christ were the greatest, gladdest adventure in life, while to them it is so hard, so trying to nerves and temper, so exasperating. Some of them drop out, some of them stagger all their life under the burden of a religion which, as Dr. Maltby once said, 'is the heaviest of all the religions in the world if you have to carry it.'

I remember going, on one occasion, to see Maskelyne and Devant's programme of illusions in London. One item was called 'The Artist's Dream.' The artist had fallen asleep in a chair near the almost completed portrait which he had been painting of his wife, who had recently died. The picture showed her seated in a swing in the garden. As the artist slept, the woman in the picture stepped down from the easel and walked across to her husband. You could see the empty swing. Then she returned and the artist awakened. The dream had been so real that he arose and took the picture down, and in front of the audience he examined it, but it was, seemingly, just an ordinary picture again. I want to say to all who are worshipping a picture of Jesus in a frame called History—to people who are beaten in their lonely toilsome effort to be like the Hero of that picture—that there is a richer experience than they have yet known. If they will sit down quietly He will come out of the picture into their life. A little faith—that kind of effortless prayer which is the leaving of the heart's door upon the latch—and the Guest will come as often as you want Him, and you will be carried further than a whole year of fussy striving would take you; for He is not a ghost of the dead past, but a friend alive for evermore.

For some people Jesus is imprisoned in forms of words. I was talking to a university student some time ago, and we spoke very frankly about Jesus; and then suddenly he said, 'But are we allowed to think that?' I said, 'Why not?' 'Well,' he said, 'I don't think it is in any of the creeds or confessions of faith or articles.' We have to be careful here. Some people feel that to go outside the language of the creeds, or outside the beliefs expressed in them, is a very doubtful procedure.

In the first place, we ought to have a reverence for creeds and confessions of faith. My own regard for them is a regard for very interesting and impressive museum specimens. In the creeds I find museum specimens of what men used to think about God and His Son many years ago. Men had to use words to express their beliefs, and they used words so carefully that some people can still recite the creeds to-day if they make one or two private interpretations, and one or two, more or less honest, mental reservations. But it would be very wrong to bind people so that they could not go beyond these ways of thinking. And it would be as futile as binding a chemist to the atomic law of Dalton, or an astronomer to the Ptolemaic theory of the planetary movements. Indeed, what should we think of a chemist who would not relinquish Dalton's law even though it no longer met the facts? What should we think of a slavish belief in atoms when the phenomena now observable demanded a belief in electrons? But, worse still, what should we think of a chemist who in his heart believed in electrons, but who, in order not to upset the old-fashioned prejudices of the few remaining orthodox, still spoke of atoms? This sort of attitude would rapidly reduce chemistry to the kind of chaos to which mathematics would be brought if, to use Oliver Wendell Holmes's simile, the figure two meant two to you, twenty-two to me, and two hundred to some one else. Theology is in danger of being just in such a muddle because we will not boldly face facts and make such new theories as are necessary, expressing those theories by saying what we mean in words which mean what they say. What have scientific thinkers done in all ages? They have gone to the facts, and then framed their beliefs, or creeds, accordingly. And they have thrown aside such theories as no longer fit the facts. That is what Jesus Himself would have us do. He did not say, 'Believe this of Me first'; He said, 'Follow Me!' and men did that, and then made their creeds. God does not want us to juggle with our minds, but to love the Lord our God with all our minds. 'I believe in one Lord Jesus Christ, the only-begotten Son of God, Begotten of His Father before all worlds, God of God, Light of Light, Very God of very God, Begotten, not made . . .' These words may express an august truth about Jesus; but, if Jesus is not real to you, He will not become real if you begin there. I think you will have to begin where the disciples began, with a daily friendship into which they entered very quietly and humbly, until the more august truths became true for them. If you begin at the wrong end because people tell you you must believe what the creeds say, you will have a figment of imagination, a ghost instead of a friend.

There is another way in which words imprison Christ. Do we not in religion use phrases which once meant a very great deal; which once were turned out red hot from the furnace of thought, but which now have lost their first meaning and their first heat? To use words which no longer mean what they say or say what we mean, is to obscure reality and to be mentally dishonest. My wife is my greatest friend and the greatest friend of my children, but we do not use identical language about her. If I spoke of her I should use words that fitted my experience of her, and my children would do the same. To do otherwise would make for unreality. So I must use about the greatest

Friend of humanity words which express my experience of Him. I must not make our relationship unreal by using words about Him which, however true for others, are not true for me. That is to make Him a ghost, not a friend. It is because this mistake has been made that people deceive themselves into supposing that they have had an experience of Jesus, which, in truth, has never been theirs. We must ask of all forms of words what they mean, and whether they express what is true *for us* about Jesus.

I think extremism in ritual makes Jesus unreal, though its purpose is to make Him real. I am helped in church services by beautiful architecture, beautiful music, stained-glass windows, and other artistic aids to worship. If you knelt during the prayers, I should like you the better for it. If you bow at the name of Jesus because it really does make you bow your whole soul before Him, I, for one, shall never criticize you. If you make the sign of the Cross because you want to remind yourself of His utter sacrifice, then do so as long as you need to. I confess I should like to have a cross in view of the congregation in my church, so that, however badly I preached, *something* would remind people of Him. I should not feel that it was popish to have candles burning on an altar if they reminded one poor soul of the Light of the World. I love everything in church ritual which really does remind me of Jesus, just as I love books or photographs or letters which remind me of my lesser friends; but if you tell me that the wafer on the altar is the actual body of Christ, a sense of unreality comes in. I ask myself what Peter might have said if he had attended Mass and then been told that the wafer was really part of the body of his Master. Does your ritual make Jesus a ghost or a friend? That seems to me the test question. And Transubstantiation seems to me as crude as the attempts of modern Spiritualism to materialize a ghost.

A friend of mine once attended a Roman Catholic service in which the priest argued for the literal presence of Christ's body in the consecrated wafer on the altar. After the service the visitor talked with one of the worshippers and asked him if he believed all that the priest had claimed. The worshipper, who was an old man, said something like this: 'When I come to Mass, sir, I cannot follow what they do up at the altar. I just kneel down and think about Jesus. I think of that last week with His friends, and the last supper; how He knelt in agony in Gethsemane; how they arrested Him and all night tortured Him, and how He died. . . .' And the old man's eyes filled with tears. 'I get very near to Jesus then, sir, and when I go home I feel that He comes with me.' The old man didn't find a value in the Mass as such. He just knelt down in that quiet place and opened his heart in prayer, and his Friend came right in. Jesus stepped out from among the tombs of dead years, out of the ghostly mists of strange rites, out of the haunted ruins built of ancient language and half-meaningless words—alive, vivid, present, royal, radiant, real. Is Jesus *real* to you?

On the two occasions when the disciples thought Jesus was a ghost, His method of self-vindication was the same. In the first instance (Matt. xiv. 26) He answered their terror with the words, 'It is I; be not afraid.' Impulsive Peter answered, 'Lord, if it be Thou, bid me come to Thee on the water.' And Jesus said, 'Come!' In the second (Luke xxiv. 37), when 'they were terrified and affrighted, and supposed that they beheld a spirit,' He said, 'Why are ye troubled? See my hands and feet that it is I Myself. Handle Me and see.' In both cases it is the same treatment. 'Put Me to the test.' The way of argument is irrelevant and impossible. The way of experience is certain. Try it. Sit down quietly for ten minutes every day for a month. Let your mind go out to Jesus. Think about Him. Believe that what He once was He eternally is. What He was for men and women years ago, He is for you to-day. All His followers would guarantee that you will find Him no ghost, but a Friend; no mere memory of long ago, but a living personal Saviour whose friendship will transform your whole nature. The very Christ of History who came to men across the troubled waters of the Galilean lake will become the Christ of Experience and come to you across the troubled waters of your twentieth-century life, with His soul-rejuvenating cry, 'Courage; it is I'; and, 'as an ineffable mystery, you shall learn in your own experience who He is.'

IV

THE INTIMACY OF THE FRIENDSHIP

The sweetest wife on sweetest marriage-day,—
  Their souls at grapple in mid-way,—
    Sweet to her sweet may say:

'I take you to my inmost heart, my true!'
  Ah, fool! but there is one heart you
    Shall never take him to!

The hold that falls not when the town is got,
  The heart's heart, whose immurèd plot
    Hath keys yourself keep not!

Its ports you cannot burst—you are withstood—
  For him that to your listening blood
    Sends precepts as he would.

Its gates are deaf to Love, high summoner;
  Yea, Love's great warrant runs not there;
    You are your prisoner.

Yourself are with yourself the sole consortress
  In that unleaguerable fortress;
    It knows you not for portress.

Its keys are at the cincture hung of God;
  Its gates are trepidant to His nod;
    By Him its floors are trod.

And if His feet shall rock those floors in wrath,
  Or blest aspersion sleek His path,
    Is only choice it hath.

Yea, in that ultimate heart's occult abode
  To lie as in an oubliette of God,
    Or in a bower untrod.

Built by a secret Lover for His Spouse;—
  Sole choice is this your life allows. . . .

FRANCIS THOMPSON.

IV

THE INTIMACY OF THE FRIENDSHIP

FRANCIS THOMPSON in his poem 'A Fallen Yew' has indicated with penetrating insight the fact that there is an inner citadel in the secret place of every man's personality to which no one but God ever obtains access; that, however willing, man cannot throw open that last door—

> The heart's heart, whose immurèd plot
> Hath keys yourself keep not! . . .
> Its keys are at the cincture hung of God.

So that, if God does not pass into it, a man is, in a real sense, a prisoner even to himself, for he is not in the position of porter at the gate; it is part of himself that is 'that unleaguerable fortress.' There does seem good reason to believe that however we confess and pour out our heart to another, keeping nothing back, he cannot enter into the very deepest place of our life. Words cannot quite make him see as we see. Words, in fact, cannot quite say *all* we mean. The outpouring may be very valuable; but the most intimate friendships must, I think, leave one inner door of which only God carries the key.

Now we shall find that a few thoughts regarding the nature of an intimate human friendship will light up for us the nature of the friendship of Jesus. Some people are very hazy about the latter. They half long for a sign of some kind to be apprehended by the senses. We religious teachers lead them into this, in a way, because in speaking about the friendship of Jesus we are bound to use human figures of speech, and we talk about seeing Him, hearing His voice, feeling His touch on our spirits, and so on. And some wistful people say to themselves, 'Well, I never feel that, or hear anything.' A good many people suspect the authenticity of their religious experience because they do not understand the signs of intimacy in friendship.

Let us, then, begin with the intimate human friendship. Our friendship with Jesus presents difficulty largely because that friendship is with an unseen person, and ordinary methods of intercommunication do not pertain. This difficulty begins to vanish when we realize that an intimate human friendship is, in a real sense, friendship with an unseen person, and the ways of communicating through eye and ear and hand, are not the most intimate ways. What does this mean? It means that if a friendship really is intimate between man and man, or man and woman, that part of it which is a kind of exchange between two seen persons is as nothing compared with the same interchange between their deeper selves. My intimate friend does not only know my outward life—what I do, the games I play, the books I read, the things in which I am interested. He knows my inward unseen life, the life that I never show another. The point is illustrated when—as the late Professor W. J. Moulton once pointed out—a man falls in love with a girl, and the critic says, 'I can't see what he can see in her.' Of course not. No statement could be more literally true. But what the critic cannot see the lover can, because the lover is in communion with an unseen person. Moreover, just because the intimacy is so deep as to be invisible to the world, it cannot be adequately carried on by those methods which are enough for the superficial friendship. Seeing, touching, hearing, are not the only means lovers know of communion. There is, with all real friends, the kind of communion of spirit which can be expressed only in long silences, when soul to some extent does seem to penetrate soul. Lovers know that the loved one understands their hidden ideals, longings, aspirations, as no one else does.

We must make room for the thought that communion with God is planned at an even greater depth of the personality. The friendship of Jesus with men on ordinary levels, in the days of His flesh, was necessary to establish the fact of the reality of the friendship of God; but when Jesus had schooled them, as He did in the appearances after the Resurrection, beyond the need of ear and eye and hand, then continual 'appearances' became unnecessary, for He could do as much, and more, for them unseen. And this is true to-day. If Jesus constantly appeared to us now, not only, I am afraid, should we be incredulous, but we should tend to think of the friendship as existing on the shallower levels of intercourse, whereas, as we have seen, the deepest friendships of all are those which function in the unseen parts of the personalities; and God, unseen, inaudible, and intangible, *and only so*, can enter into His own secret dwelling within us of which He alone has the key. We must cease then, to think of our friendship with Jesus in the terms of mere acquaintanceships, for He comes to us below the levels plumbed by our most intimate friends.

This supplies the answer to those who still seek a sign of the authenticity of their experience of Christ's friendship, and who say, 'I am never quite sure whether I get communion with Him or not.' Let us ask what are the signs of our deepest human friendships. Is the best sign of a great friendship a friend's response to what we ask, or his response to something the friendship is? For example, ask yourself this question: If my friend's mother in a distant town falls ill and he urgently desires to visit her, which would reveal deeper friendship—my lending him my motor-bike in response to his request for it, or my taking it to his door for him as soon as I heard of the need, without waiting to be asked? In the first case there has to be a request made with a voice. But in the second the fact of the friendship creates in me a longing to help. The first illustrates the communion between two persons on what we might call the level of the seen; but the second illustrates the communion, at a deeper level, of two persons on what we may call the level of the unseen.

So it seems to me a sign of the reality of the

friendship of Jesus if the very friendship, kept fresh by prayer, worship, and communion, creates in me a longing to do His will. We ought to train ourselves to perceive His comings into our deeper life, the communion of His unseen with our unseen, by watching our thought, feeling, and will, which, as every one in these psychological days is tired of hearing, are the three indivisible parts of the human personality. If I have a thought, as I go about my work, which is high and lofty and liberating, with no meanness in it, I ought to say to myself, 'The Friend has visited me to-day; He has touched my thoughts.' If I find my feeling widening so that bitterness is purged right away, and I am possessed of a large sympathy, a broad tolerance, a deep brotherliness for all men, then I ought to teach myself to say, 'The Friend has been near my feeling to-day.' If I find myself no longer shrinking from the unwelcome task, telling myself that in Him I am adequate for anything that may make a demand upon me, then I may say to myself, 'The very fact that "I cannot" has become "I can," and "I can" has become "I will," means that the Friend has been near my will to-day.' In this way we shall come to know how very often He is near, and we shall make the friendship a reality. If some one says, 'But the heathen have this enlargement of thought, feeling, and will,' that is not, in my view, an objection. It only shows that God is near them also. I am friendly to people who never think of me as their friend; but this does not lessen the reality of my friendship to those with whom I can be more intimate. Hundreds of people pray almost daily, 'O Lord be with me to-day,' or 'Let Thy presence be manifest amongst us all.' Yet they hardly know what they mean, or what they expect to happen, or how they expect God to manifest His presence. Some half hope for an outward sign, others look for 'a feeling in the meeting,' and it would be cruel to suppose that either desire is not legitimate, or that both have not again and again manifested the Presence Divine. But the amazing experience of the transforming friendship we may have with Jesus applies to everyday life, and we must see the signs of its reality, not, as Browning would say, 'by a comet's rush, but a rose's birth'; not in the unusual, or the spectacular, but in the quiet daily growth and blossoming of our own personality.

There is one great thing that this intimate friendship with Christ, if cultivated, will do for us. It will reveal hidden motives and semi-repressed desires. Spiritual health does depend on our knowing ourselves. Frank conversation with a friend will take us part of the way. Confession to a minister who understands, whose very training and experience have made him a doctor of souls, and whose vows make it impossible for him ever to betray a confidence, helps many people. In serious cases what is known as psycho-analysis may be necessary. But none of these ways is to become habitual. It should be habitual, however, and part of the living friendship of the soul with Christ that we should regularly go into the silence where He is, and very quietly undergo the process which Charles Wesley has perfectly described in his hymn, 'Open, Lord, my inward ear.'

> Show me, as my soul can bear,
> The depth of inbred sin;
> All the unbelief declare,
> The pride that lurks within;
> Take me, whom Thyself hast bought,
> Bring into captivity
> Every high aspiring thought
> That would not stoop to Thee.

And in that quiet place we are to question all our motives: Am I doing this work because I want to serve God, or am I doing it so as to come into the limelight and satisfy my instinct for self-display? Am I doing this rescue-work or reading these books, in order that I may face the realities of life, or in order to satisfy a morbid curiosity and a perverted instinct? Am I doing this or that, whether it be the way I dress or the way in which I speak or the friends I make, with clean motives behind me, or is my motive a murky fear concerned with what others might think or say? Am I giving money to this fund because that money is an expression of personality and because I want to help a great cause, or because I want to see my name high up on the subscription list? Am I working for that degree because I desire to undertake a mental discipline and fit myself the better for service, or is it to put letters after my name and assume superiority over others? Am I fighting in this or that cause because it is just and right, or to cloak my passion for pugnacity? Am I staying at home really to look after mother or because I am not strong, or is it because I shrink from facing up to life, because I am too big a baby to make good in some profession or sphere of service? Is my motive pure altruism in this or that matter, or do I long to be called 'unselfish'?

What we call quiet self-examination in the presence of Christ—the attempt to see ourselves as He sees us—ends in His showing us ourselves as we really are. He is not so poor a friend that He blazons our failings in letters of fire on the wall when we ask our friends to supper, but if we will go into some place of sanctuary and sit down quietly for a little while with the outer door upon the latch, He will come right through, and undo the inner one for Himself and us, and in the intimacy of friendship, in the kindly, inexorable ways of perfect Love, He will reveal to us something of our poverty, unworthiness, and shame. But He will do more than this. Our secret citadel is His holy place, and He had always a passion to cleanse His own temple. All evil intentions and thoughts and desires fly from His searching glance as bats fly from a dungeon when it is opened to the blaze of day. And instead of them there shall dwell the sunshine of His glory, the radiance of His abiding presence, and the strength of His ineffable peace.

V

THE INEXORABLE NATURE OF THE FRIENDSHIP

Jesus, whose lot with us was cast,
Who saw it out, from first to last:
Patient and fearless, tender, true,
Carpenter, vagabond, felon, Jew:
Whose humorous eye took in each phase
Of full rich life this world displays,
Yet evermore kept fast in view
The far-off goal it leads us to:
Who, as your hour neared, did not fail—
The world's fate trembling in the scale—
With your half-hearted band to dine,
And chat across the bread and wine,
Then went out firm to face the end,
Alone, without a single friend:
Who felt, as your last words confessed,
Wrung from a proud unflinching breast
By hours of dull ignoble pain,
Your whole life's fight was fought in vain:
Would I could win, and keep, and feel
That heart of love, that spirit of steel.

Lines published anonymously in the *Spectator*, but since traced to DR. WILFRED BRINTON, who gave his life to slum work.

V

THE INEXORABLE NATURE OF THE FRIENDSHIP

I think I never was at any time
A Christian, as you nickname all the world.

So Guido, in 'The Ring and the Book.' I wonder if it *is* a nickname rather than a true description. I wonder whether Peter would recognize me as a follower of Christ in the sense in which he understood the term after the Resurrection. And I wonder whether what we have produced is really Christianity at all, or something quite different—not nearly so strenuous, not nearly so austere, not nearly so beautiful.

I am not chanting the dirge that the Churches have failed. We can leave that to the man who is hard up for an excuse for playing golf on Sundays, or for having nothing to do with the Church. Any fool can stand outside a thing and pull it down. The people who care are inside trying to build up. They are far more conscious of the disparity between dream and actuality; but all the folk with any grit are still working to make the dream come true. Yet the dirge is just true enough to hurt the people who care. Is the trouble that the real thing has not been tried yet? Is it that we have tried not Christianity but the bogus substitute? *Are we expecting to see the results without having kept the rules?* Are we expecting to see the glorious fruits of Christianity grow from something that is not Christianity at all? Bring it down from generalities: Am I really a Christian? Am I fulfilling the conditions necessary to the results? What are the conditions? Jesus left us in no doubt about that. 'Whosoever will come after Me, let him renounce himself, and take up his cross, and follow Me.' The earliest Gospel gives us that, and the others all repeat it. No reporter missed that word. As Matthew Arnold observed, 'There is no other maxim of Jesus which has such a combined stress of evidence for it, and may be taken as so eminently His.'

I am afraid we have not fulfilled the conditions. Religion has become a soft and flabby and aesthetic thing. An effeminate thing. Truly regarded, it claims only the heroic spirits, men and women. Look at the kind of people Christianity has mastered through all history. It calls to sacrifice, peril, adventure, and risk. Christianity is not a friendly society, much less a friendly society floated on tea. Its symbol is not a cushion, but a cross. A Cross! What do any of us know of a cross? People talk about bearing their cross when they mean getting on with their mother-in-law, or bearing a twinge of rheumatism that they get through coming home from the pictures in the wet. A cross! A cross is a bloody thing. But Jesus uses the word. And He uses it of *all* who would follow Him. He uses it of me and of you. He invites us to a friendship, but its demands are inexorable.

Most of us are not unlike the disciples before the Cross became real. They played at this new religion.

It was infinitely attractive to their well-developed Jewish instincts. It was pleasant to be spoken of as a friend of this wonderful Teacher on whose lips multitudes hung day after day. How popular He was! Besides, there were great promises made to them which they thought of in terms of material reward. 'Ye shall sit upon twelve thrones . . . and every one that hath forsaken houses . . . shall receive an hundredfold, and shall inherit eternal life.' It was a sound investment, and a Jew wouldn't miss that.

Then, high up in the air, a gossamer net began to be weaved over His head. It seemed no more than a cobweb. But it was made of suspicion, and distrust, and jealousy, and hatred, and abuse, and bitterness. It came lower and seemed made of thread; then lower and seemed to be made of cord; then lower and seemed to be made of rope. 'And certain of them that were with Him walked no more with Him.' It came lower and lower and lower, till *it was seen to be made of steel cable.* And then it fell. And it caught only one Man, the only perfect Christian in the world's history. 'For they all forsook Him and fled.' And they hid in the garden, some of them, all night.

And then, from their hiding-places among the olives in the garden, they looked, late the next day, across the valley, and the sky was strangely dark for midday. Behind the contour of the hills was one blood-red streak of light, like a wound in something sentient. And black against that red they saw two crosses raised. And they remembered that two thieves were to be crucified. But then a third raised its hideous form against the wounded, spurious night. . . . Words came back to them, slowly, but dropping like molten lead on a naked brain : 'The Son of Man must suffer many things . . . and be crucified. . . .' Then down the hillside they went, stumbling through the jungly undergrowth, tripping on the roots of olives, blinded by tears, shaken with sobs. They crossed the brook Kidron. Joined by women, they climbed the dreadful place of the skull. They looked. Yes, it was He. They knelt. They never ran away again. They understood the word 'Cross' then. They realized how much the friendship which had transformed them might cost them. They understood the conditions He had laid down. They accepted them. They became Christians for the first time, in the only place where a man ever does become a Christian. And because they began to fulfil the conditions the results began to accrue. Pentecost—and all the world upside down, and themselves *drunk*—with the wine of a new life.

We are all attracted by Christ, but we are held back by a thousand things. One of them is that we are afraid what people would think of us if we went all the way. There is not one person reading these words who does not know in his soul that he would be a far better man if he did not care what people thought of him. Some people lie awake at night worrying about what other people say and think of them. We are little puppy-dogs led about on the string of what our business friends would think, and what our social friends would think, and what our relatives would think, and what Mrs. Huggins opposite would think, until in the end we care more for what they all think than what the eternal Christ thinks.

But He took a line of action that made His own mother think He was mad. He held convictions, and lived up to them, which made people call Him fool, fanatic, crank. And He was a sensitive soul. It made Him feel very lonely. Probably none of us can help *feeling* what people say. But Jesus never let what people thought sway Him one hair-breadth from His chosen path—not even what His mother and brethren and friends said. Men have had the V.C. for less bravery than that attitude manifests. I say to myself that I am not a Christian. I know that I am not fit to be His friend. But that is the way He calls. And it isn't a lonely way any longer. He walked it. He walks it still with every man who is man enough to follow. Only we must not say that above all things we must be conventional or respectable. For He says we must be sincere above all things.

Another thing that keeps us back is that we are not willing to have our prayers answered. We pray as the disciples did before they were Christians. 'Give me . . .' And Jesus says still, 'Are you willing to drink the cup that I drink?' We ask for results. He says, 'Are you prepared to keep the rules?' Do we ask to know the will of God, without being prepared to follow it? Do we ask for strength to follow Christ, counting not His lonely way, His utter sacrifice, His breaking heart? Do we ask to be made pure, and then clasp the rags of our impurity yet tighter to us? Do we ask for victory over temptation, and then love our hateful little sins more than victory over them? Do we ask to see His face, not realizing that if He answered the prayer the vision would scorch our petty souls? Yes, we do. We are afraid that if He answered our prayers He might make us more than we dare to be. And every time a man prays, 'Give me . . .' Jesus answers, 'Are you willing . . .?'

Another thing that keeps us back is that we too often keep one eye on the prospect of getting something out of Christianity—just as the disciples did before they became Christians. 'I don't go to church now,' says a man; 'the parson can't preach for nuts; and I'm not getting anything out of it.' Imagine a Tommy sitting on the fire-step smoking a 'Ruby Queen' at the moment when his pals were just preparing to go over the top. The sergeant comes along and says, 'What are you doing?' (Only he puts it better than that.) 'Oh,' says the man, 'I'm going home; I'm not getting anything out of this war.' I am afraid the air would be blue. Perhaps navy blue! Some one pointed out in a volume of essays written during the war that a man who joined up to get something out of it would be rightly considered half-witted. Well, the Church—which is only another word for the organized friends of Jesus—is a great army fighting the most tremendous battle in the world. Even the disciples did not get much out of it when they were always squabbling about what they were going to *get*. (' Who shall sit on Thy right hand . . . ? ') They got most out of it when they put most into it, when they were missionaries in the heathen world for Christ's sake. (' They departed from the presence of the council, rejoicing that they were counted worthy to suffer shame for the Name.)

Amusements in the Church are well enough if they are a part of the fellowship of the Church, but not if they are used to attract the outsider. They give him a wrong conception of what it means to be a friend of Jesus. He takes all the Church ' gives,' and asks what more you are prepared to do to keep him. If we made the threshold higher —and Jesus made it very high—men would think it more worth while to join. I confess to being afraid of this pandering. I suppose I am narrow-minded, but sometimes, when I hear the constant rattling of teacups at this social and at that, I seem to hear the quiet voice of One who, while He made merry at a wedding-feast, said also, ' Are you willing to drink the cup that I drink ? '

Garibaldi's words, often quoted, yet do breathe the spirit of Christ. It is the big demand that makes the heroic spirit. It is the untamed jungle that makes the pioneer. It is the untraversed, perilous journey that makes the explorer. It is the big task that makes the big soul. Christ's challenge, it seems to me, is that we should go into training so as to become fit—fit for the Kingdom of God. If you were playing football for England to-morrow, you wouldn't be up till midnight to-night eating doughnuts and jam-puffs and meringues. You would do everything to be at your best, and then you would not need evidences of the ability of England to play. You would be one of the evidences yourself. Christ asks for nothing less. There are certain kinds of plays and pictures and books and jokes and friendships; no one will criticize you for having anything to do with them. Leave them to the touchline people who criticize the players, wear warm overcoats, smoke fat cigars, and deceive themselves that they are sportsmen. Christ wants you to keep fit, to play the game, to be an athlete, and to lay aside everything that might steal away your fitness for the greatest, and therefore the most strenuous, game in the world. And you will not need evidences of the power of Christianity. You will become one yourself. Such people are real Christians, and there is no dirge about *their* Christianity failing. It's the most glorious thing in the world.

When Jesus ascended, though He still had only a handful of followers, He was well content. For every one of them was 'all-out' for His kingdom. Every one was a picked friend ready to make the coming of His kingdom the first passionate purpose of life. There are enough people in the world who call themselves by Christ's name to win it all for Him, given only the willingness to accept all the implications of this inexorable friendship whatever it may cost. And Jesus on the way to His Cross, whispers His question still, 'Are you willing to drink the cup that I drink, and to go all the way with Me?'

VI

THE QUALIFICATIONS OF THE FRIEND

My humanity is the way by which men must travel.

SUSO.

His life was gentle, and the elements
So mixed in him that Nature might stand up
And say to all the world 'This was a man!'

SHAKESPEARE:
Julius Caesar.

I never realized God's birth before—
How He grew likest God in being born.

BROWNING:
'The Ring and the Book'
(Pompilia, 1690–1).

To have to do with nothing but the true,
The good, the eternal,—and these, not alone
In the main current of the general life,
But small experiences of every day,
Concerns of the particular hearth and home:
To learn not only by a comet's rush
But a rose's birth—not by the grandeur, God,
But the comfort, Christ.

BROWNING:
'The Ring and the Book'
(Giuseppe Caponsacchi, 2089–97).

VI

THE QUALIFICATIONS OF THE FRIEND

It is a very significant thing that Jesus had one favourite title for Himself, 'the Son of Man.' It is used over eighty times in the New Testament, and yet the Evangelists themselves never use it of Jesus, nor does any one ever address Him by that name. He uses it of Himself, and no one uses it save He. The reason of this reluctance on the part of the Gospel writers is not far to seek. The title emphasized His humanity. Whatever His followers thought of Him during His sojourn with them, when some of them came to write down their records of that life, that death, and that after-death, they desired not to stress His humanity, but what had meantime become for them a certainty, that He was divine.

Now Jesus, by the use of this very title and His emphasis on it, insisted that He was a man. I do not think we need say that the title was an echo of Daniel. I do not think it implied Messiahship. Jesus seems very rarely to have implied that. The use of the title was a deliberate emphasis on the most inspiring fact of all human history, namely, that this radiant, vivid, powerful, humble personality, so gloriously alive, so perfectly happy, was, and is for ever, man. In Him all the possibilities of manhood were gathered together and harmoniously realized.

We must guard ourselves from any mistaken idea that this constitutes a denial of divinity. For too long we have set the ideas of divinity and humanity over against one another in separate categories of thought, and felt that what we allowed to the one we must subtract from the other. Nor must we think of divinity in terms of the marvellous, like the little girl to whom her mother tried to explain the thought of God dwelling within her. She looked up and said, 'But, mummy, if God is in me, why can't I do tricks?' I do not think any reputable theologian would try to prove the divinity of Jesus from His miracles. To do that is to find oneself in a quandary when new knowledge brings such actions as Jesus gloriously wrought within the power of men to-day, as is doubtless speedily happening, just as Jesus Himself foresaw. The manifestations of divinity are to be looked for along the lines of the quality of character; not in might, but in goodness; not in the uncanny, but in moral splendour. It may be that, if again a man lived on such a high plane and in such close communion with God, the incidents of Christ's life might represent normal activity; and divinity itself is not to be thought of as necessarily in a different category from humanity, for perfect humanity may reveal divinity as fully as the latter can express itself in human life. In other words, Jesus, both in what He did and much more perfectly in what He was, does not, as it were, stand up and say, 'This is what

God can do, but man cannot.' He says, 'This is what God meant man to be and to do.' 'He that believeth on Me, the works that I do shall he do also; *and greater works than these shall he do.*' And 'ye therefore shall be perfect as your heavenly Father is perfect.' This is what Myers means in his line:

> Jesus, divinest when Thou most art man!

Divinity stands most clearly revealed and most perfectly understood in perfect humanity.

So a tremendous message stands out clear and vivid. Jesus by His insistence on His own perfect humanity is saying to us, 'This is what I made of human life. This is what you can make of it. I fought the battle and won through, with no other weapons save those which are still available for you. I have been tempted. I have lived in difficult circumstances. I have worn throbbing human flesh, and know its hot desires. I have been through pain, and sorrow, and disappointment, and loneliness, and bitter treatment, and misunderstanding. I have been persecuted by my enemies. I have been deserted by my friends. I have never been delivered from anything, nor has anything been made easy, just because I was the Son of God; but as the Son of Man I have entered into the secret of the companionship of God, who is always loving, always available, and always working for good. And I live for ever to be your Friend, your Guide, your Strength.' So He presents to us His qualifications. He is all that we long to be. Don't wrap

Him in mists of Eastern imagery! Don't say 'Oh, well, He was different.' Don't make excuses for yourself by making false statements about Him. Before ever a soul had made a single guess about His divinity, He had won the battle which takes most of us a lifetime to fight. He was a man. What a man!

I have sometimes wondered—though I have never seen it in books, and I am sure I shall be told that it is bad exegesis—whether Pilate did not have a tremendous sense of the manhood of Jesus. I like to imagine the scene. Before Pilate a crowd is gathered, with, we may suppose, the members of the Sanhedrin and their supporters in the foreground. Pilate had been beaten by them. He had been made to do something that was against his better judgement and against his finer instincts, and he had been made to do it because they frightened him into it by their talk about Caesar. This did not make him love them any more. He saw them for what they were, a mob of despicable plotters—worms rather than men. Their Victim stands beside him. What a man He was compared with His cunning, scheming enemies! Pilate, at least, did not ascribe His qualities to divinity. But how heroically He had endured His torments! His whole attitude appealed to the Roman ideal of manhood. Pilate's Roman soul was stirred. With a lashing irony which would not fail to sting the enemies whom he dared not openly flout, he makes a comparison calculated to make those wheedling, skulking, little-souled Jews—whom, with all his Roman soul, he hated—writhe with fury. He pays Jesus the tribute that He at least in his judge's eyes is every inch a man. Now, if Pilate spoke in Greek or Aramaic we are bound to translate his word as 'Behold the Man.' But what if Pilate broke into those words which the Church has always treasured, and spoke in his native Latin, '*Ecce Homo.*' Then we may as reasonably translate 'Behold, a Man!'[1] as much as to say, 'Here, at last, among all the Jews I have ever come in contact with, is a real man as a Roman thinks of men.'

Let us watch Jesus facing life, and using the weapons which are at our disposal and the resources which are available for us. The three great enemies of our personal life are temptation, worry, and fear. How does He meet them?

Temptation came to Him just as it comes to us. We need not imagine a picture of Him in the desert with some horrible devil, with claws and a tail, bending over Him. He was alone with evil suggestions thronging on to the threshold of His mind, just as they do in our case. What does He do always in temptation? He slams the door of His mind by turning away to other thoughts. To stop and argue with such thoughts is to court disaster, and to let such thoughts right into the mind is to make sure of it. As soon as a thought—and all temptation begins in the realm of the mind—is seen to be evil, slam the door and direct your thoughts elsewhere. If you are subject, as many are, to evil thoughts which haunt you, say, in the waking

[1] Notice the comma after 'Behold' in the Revised Version.

moments of the day as you lie in bed, don't lie in bed and argue with them. Jump out of bed and have a cold bath. This will slam the door of the mind against them far more easily than by staying in bed trying to say prayers. And while you bathe let the water be a symbol of the cleansing presence of God, and the day has been saved from a stain which would have spoilt it all. Watch Jesus! 'Get thee behind Me, Satan!' That's slamming the door, refusing to play with the false idea. Then His mind goes at once to other things: 'Then said Jesus unto His disciples, "If any man would come after Me . . ."'

Worry means that there is something too uncomfortable to forget, too disturbing to sink into the unconscious mind, and yet to which we will not face up, or cannot, because we cannot deal with some problems before they arise. How does Jesus face worry? In brief, and very simply, I think it is thus: He asks God what His will is in regard to the next step. And He leaves all further steps until it is time to take them. Many of us worry because we are trying to cross bridges before we get to them, before we can even see them clearly. Wherever Jesus is found praying, I believe He was asking God what was the next thing to *do*. And I believe that God will show us the next step—not the distant step, but the next step. We must take that, and then, and then only, have we qualified to ask Him about the next. Let us sit down quietly and survey the whole problem. Then ask God to show us the next step, remembering that God often speaks to us in and through the advice of a friend, through what we call common sense, as well as by the swift intuition which sometimes seems like His direct voice ; and then let us take that step, and the taking of it will draw off the energy of the mind from worrying about problems beyond the scope of any possible present action.

Fear is not, for most people, a physical thing ; though some of us have known what that is, and were glad that Jesus had passed even that way. But in this comfortable civilization physical fear plays a small part. Yet we shall need all the heroism we can muster to face the fear of what people say, what people think, and what people do. We must not let fear alter our actions. Jesus was wounded to the very soul as men dropped away and left Him. It helped to break His heart when, at the moment of greatest need, 'they all forsook Him and fled.' But it made no difference to what He did. To be perfectly accurate, fear is not in itself an evil thing. It is one of the instincts implanted by God. Without it the race would never have survived. It is one of the driving forces of the personality. To fear is not to be frightened. People who are said not to know what fear is, by that very fact do not know what courage is either. Fearlessness is allied to recklessness. I would not trust myself in a boat, or in a motor, or through a jungle, or on an operating table, or in any place of risk with a man who said he never knew what fear was. That is too cabbage-like a mentality to cope with risks and dangers. Confidence is the attribute of the man who knows fear, but knows also his own power to meet it, and is never swayed from his course by it. This is what Jesus had. He did things which would make us sweat with fear. He held convictions which made Him hated. He *was* things which made Him utterly lonely—and He was a very friend-loving, warm-hearted man. Deserted, forsaken, beaten as it seemed; cranky, odd, unconventional, eccentric, a fool—but a Master of Life, quiet and strong and happy in the depths of His soul, the one Man who was never beaten, because no one ever made Him afraid. The priests were swayed from their position by fear of what He claimed. The Pharisees were swayed from theirs by fear of the people. The mob were swayed from their former loyalty by fear of their leaders, multiplied by mob-hysteria. Pilate was swayed from duty by fear of Caesar. The disciples were swayed by fear of being made fools of. But Jesus, feeling more than they all—since the mark of rank in nature is capacity for mental pain—was swayed not one hair's-breadth from that grim, awful, holy purpose which God showed Him to be the next step, and which led Him, at last, to the place of the skull.

So the Son of God became the Son of Man that the sons of men might become the sons of God. And when I see Him meeting temptation, worry, fear, and the thousand problems of life down to its smallest and most trivial detail, I wonder that I can even pretend to be His friend. Yet He invites all who will come to Him into that amazing, transforming friendship which He is so anxious to begin, and which, once begun, He, for His part, will always refuse to end. I do not wonder at the advice of the old veteran, Paul, to the young soldier, Timothy, just starting out for the battlefield: 'Remember Jesus Christ, risen from the dead!' I pass it on to you, because, unless we had remembered it, there is not a man of us who would not have slipped back into the slime of sin till he could never raise his head again for shame. Remember Jesus Christ and His transforming friendship, and start all over again.

VII

THE INHERENT POWER OF THE FRIENDSHIP

He comes to us as One unknown, without a name, as of old by the lake-side He came to those who knew Him not. He speaks to us the same word, ' Follow thou Me,' and sets us to the task which He has to fulfil for our time. He commands. And to those who obey Him, whether they be wise or simple, He will reveal Himself in the toils, the conflicts, the sufferings which they shall pass through in His fellowship, and, as an ineffable mystery, they shall learn in their own experience Who He is.

ALBERT SCHWEITZER :
The Quest of the Historical Jesus.

VII

THE INHERENT POWER OF THE FRIENDSHIP

THE realization of any friendship means the realization of power. If two people become real friends, then, in the respects in which one is strong and the other admires that strength, that strength, through communion, will pass to the weaker. The effort of the weaker to be strong is not the most powerful agency at work. The most effective agency is the friendship itself. The two friends will tend to become like one another, and both be stronger than before. This is true whether it be the strength of evil or of good. One nature does feed on another, the weaker on the stronger, so that where one Friend is Perfect Strength we can think of all His weaker brethren feeding on Him ; a fact which we symbolize in the Holy Communion, for in communion with Jesus our very souls feed on His nature as our bodies feed on bread. He is the 'bread of God which cometh down out of heaven and giveth life unto the world.'

This kind of power, by its very nature, is one that is received gradually. Yet the very act of entry into this friendship releases at once tremendous power into the personality. The decision to be Christ's man or Christ's woman charges the soul with power. Think of the case of Matthew, who was a very ordinary person, a clerk in an office as we should say to-day, and then, to see it better, translate it into terms of modern experience. You are sitting in your office, or college, or home. An all-but-stranger calls to you, 'Follow Me!' With no question as to livelihood, with no further thought of your business, your career, the opinions of your relatives, you begin a new and strange life. As we read the story, trying to see it without the familiarity which glosses over its wonder, we are almost tempted to ask whether there was not some strange power at work on Matthew's mind. Words like 'fascination,' 'hypnotism,' 'magnetic personality,' suggest themselves; but before we seek refuge in them let us look more closely.

In all probability Matthew had heard of Jesus before. He lived at Capernaum, and Capernaum was ringing with the words and deeds of Jesus. Matthew in all probability had been attracted by the winsomeness of Christ, by His radiant joy, by His exuberant religion, by His thoughts of God and the world. Here was a Master of life. Here was a Lover of men, even men whom every one else despised, men who collected taxes from their own compatriots for the hated Roman. Maybe Matthew had stood on the outskirts of the crowds which listened to Jesus. There had been no personal, conscious relationship between himself and Christ. He had been attracted, just as so many are to-day, but not wholly won. We can imagine him saying to himself, 'I'd give anything to be like that. My whole being leaps out in response to His appeal. But I'm too old; I can't alter things now. It would make too big a revolution in my life. I must think of my prospects, of what my employers would say, of what my relatives would think. . . .' And, again like so many to-day, he had gone back to his desk, back to the old rut that would have deepened and deepened till it became the grave of his soul.

But there comes a dramatic moment which is the turning point of his career. Jesus comes right up to the desk where he sits 'at the receipt of custom.' The dim, hazy attractiveness of Christ becomes focused into one burning ray that scorches its way into his befogged soul. Man to man, face to face, heart to heart; the desire of Christ for Matthew, meeting the desire of Matthew for Christ. There in the open street they stand like two highly-charged electric terminals, and the spark passes from the higher to the lower, from the positive to the negative. 'Follow Me!' Not an invitation, nor a request, but a command. And what happened? Matthew was no longer content merely to remain attracted. He can no longer give the lie to his better self. Following Christ became the dominating purpose in life, and in that great decision there always lies power.

I have described that event in detail just because a great many people stand where Matthew stood before he met Jesus face to face. No one can help being attracted to Jesus; no one can help loving Him in a kind of vague and general way. We've all said, 'Yes, it's all very beautiful. I'd give anything to be an out-and-outer ; but . . . I should have to give up some of my pleasures, and it would interfere with my comfortable way . . . and people would think me goody-goody.' So we give up the idea. We are still on His side if it doesn't interfere with the even tenor of our way. We are shocked at wickedness, of course, but equally 'of course' one must wink at some things. We should vote for Christ if it came to that, but we should conceal our voting-papers from our fashionable and business friends. So we hide under the words 'impracticable,' 'hopelessly idealistic,' 'later on, perhaps'; and many of us will continue to hide under them till the Angel of Death tears off the filthy clothes of our self-excusing, and we stand stark naked before the white throne of God.

Let us see how the decision to make the friendship of Christ the dominating purpose in life brings power to the soul. In the first place, a great decision settles a whole lot of lesser issues without any conflict of the mind. You decide to come to church. The decision by itself settles small issues. The very fact that you have made the decision ends the conflict in the mind that may have been ranging round the advantages of going for a walk. You do not say to yourself, 'Now, shall I take a hat? Shall I go up this street or up that?' The greater decision means that you do a whole lot of lesser things without the fatigue of making further choices. This means power. Weakness is with those in whose minds there is continual conflict. Ought I to do this? Dare I do that? Shall I follow this, or that? While we are weighing two courses in the mind, and are unresolved, we are weak. We are like a fellow who cannot make up his mind what to be. First his mind follows the advantages of this profession, then of that. And as long as he is in that state he will do no good. To make a decision for Christ means that one will not always be worrying 'Is it right to do that? Is it wrong to do this?' The great decision will carry with it the resolving of a thousand lesser issues; and that means power, for it saves the expenditure of energy on lesser decisions. The definite decision to be Christ's man *first*, enables a man to throw the whole bias of his mind into the higher course, and saves him the exhausting process of weighing one course against another.

In the second place, that personal decision spells power because it is behind, and gives meaning to, incidents of life which without it would be meaningless and monotonous. When to be a worthy friend of Jesus becomes the dominant purpose of a man's life, it runs through every part of his life as the thread runs through a necklace and gives the smallest bead a place, a meaning, and a value. Without it, life's happenings are scattered as beads on a bedroom floor. But the thread of purpose gathers them up and makes them all—however apparently trivial—part of one great whole.

There were a few nurses during the war who had no thought of making nursing, even for the war's duration, a great dominating purpose in life. They joined up in a moment of emotional impulse, and after they had been photographed in their uniforms there didn't seem to them to be anything to do but flirt, and hope for the end of the war. The routine bored them. The discipline chafed them. Even the uniform very soon irked them. But to most nurses that great, glorious purpose ran like a gold thread through every part of their work. It gave colour and meaning and importance to the most trivial and repellent task. They were helping in the glorious task of reducing suffering to a minimum. They belonged to one of the most glorious professions in the world. And from personal experience I may say that the patients found no difficulty in placing their nurses in the correct category. And the man who says, 'From to-day I am Christ's friend,' finds a thread running through every part of his life. All its monotonies and drudgeries are caught up and sanctified. Or, to change the figure, every little wave on the beach has the throb of the mighty ocean behind it.

In the third place, it may truly be said that if behind the great dominating purpose there is the dynamic power of an instinctive emotion, then the human personality realizes a degree of power which is unknown under any other conditions. Let us illustrate this. One has heard of the old gentleman walking serenely in the country when he discovers a raging bull tearing down the lane behind him. He leaps over a fence which, both before and after, he finds an almost insuperable difficulty in negotiating. There was a great dominating purpose to save his skin, and it was fired by the instinctive emotion of fear. But let us go further. If the purpose is altruistic, then the power released is greater still. You are lying in bed on Sunday morning. You argue that wild horses would not get you up. There is a cry of fire, and you are at the end of the garden in five seconds. But if some one tells you that your child is still imprisoned in the burning building, what happens? Blinding smoke, scorching flame, falling timber cannot keep you out. A new power is released which is even greater than before. First, there was a dominating purpose to save the skin, released by the emotion of fear. But second, there was a dominating altruistic purpose fired by the emotion of love, and that power is a thousand times greater.

This is good psychology, but it is also very good religion. To be the friend of Jesus means that you join in that great altruistic purpose for which Jesus called His friends together at the first. And it is fired by the greatest emotion ever set free on this earth—the love of Jesus. 'The love of Christ constraineth us.' The superman is not the man of iron of whom we sometimes foolishly dream. He is the man who has at heart the greatest purpose ever launched on this earth—the coming of God's Kingdom—and whose soul is fired by the great passion of a real love of Christ. Nothing can beat that power. Wesley sets before his helpers the great altruistic purpose of the evangelization of England. He calls forth the emotion of the fear of God. England is evangelized. Wilberforce sets before his workers the great altruistic dominating purpose of liberty for the slaves. He kindles it with the emotion of pity. Slavery is abolished. Jesus, greatest Leader of all, sets before His friends the great altruistic dominating purpose of the conquest of sin and the establishment of God's Kingdom, and fires it with love, and, if we were worth calling His friends, the whole world would be the garden of God in this generation.

And what does He ask of me now? It cannot be too often emphasized that Christianity is essentially the most tremendous loyalty to Jesus Christ of which our personality is capable. Don't start by *trying to be good*! Start by being the friend of Jesus and you will become good. 'Follow Me'—and that is all He asks. No one knows what 'being good' is or means apart from Him. In Him all hard, cold, marble ethics become changed, like Pygmalion's statue, into the warm, living, breathing Jesus, whom we can follow and love and adore.

It sometimes seems to me as though there are only three courses a man can take in life. He is like a ship on the ocean, an ocean dark and restless, with mysterious tides, brooding tempests, strange currents, and ever the cruel rocks from which the Sirens call. He can steer straight for the rocks. Very few do that, though some do so because the Sirens are too much for them. Many take the second course—they decide to drift. And let it be clearly seen that that is just as much a decision as any other. Then, after they have visited the ports of sin, they may take the Pilot on board and conceive the hope that somehow they may find the harbour at sunset. And some do when 'all is but a wreck.' It is a poor return to make of our personality to God.

There is a far finer choice than that. It is to take the Pilot on board in all the glory and purity of life's golden morning; not when sin has been tasted, and turned to dust and ashes in the mouth; not when desire—which seems as beautiful as a child's soap bubble till we grasp it and find only a wet mess in the palm of our hand—has left us more hungry, restless, and dissatisfied than before; not when all the ports of evil have been visited and found to be no true harbour of the spirit; but to sail with Christ with all the kingdoms of this world in sight, while life is young and fresh and beautiful.

Thus to love, thus to serve, thus to follow, thus to sail in unknown seas with the breath of life in one's nostrils, the wine of life in one's lips, the joy of life in one's heart; this is to find what life is, and why man was created in the morning of the world, when all the stars of God sang together; this is to find the joy Christ had—a joy unquenchable through all the sorrows of His earthly voyaging; this is to find what Paul meant by the 'glorious liberty of the children of God.' This is life. This is conquest. This is adventure. This is religion.

VIII

THE PERSONAL NATURE OF THE FRIENDSHIP

The Son of God who loved me, and gave Himself up for me.

St. Paul.

I felt that I did trust in Christ, Christ alone for salvation; and an assurance was given me that He had taken away *my* sins, even *mine*, and saved *me* from the law of sin and death.

John Wesley.

VIII

THE PERSONAL NATURE OF THE FRIENDSHIP

THERE is a very true, and, I think, justifiable sense in which the supremely important things in life are the personal things, the things that touch *us*. For instance, if you have been up for an important examination, and the day arrives for the lists to be published, you do not rush to the college notice-board to see if John Smith has passed, or if Mary Huggins has come through all right. You look for *your* name. And no one in the world would call that selfishness.

I have read of a man who was once having his breakfast with the morning paper propped up against the teapot. His wife was upstairs with a little lassie who was ill. The man read the story of some Armenian atrocities. Men had been murdered, women outraged, little children flung into rivers. The man went on munching toast, and when he had finished he went off to the office. Nor do I mean to imply any censure of his attitude. During the day the silent angel whom some call the Angel of Death, and others, who know, the Angel of Love, came to his house, and so quietly touched that little golden-haired form that had slept in the cot near his bed for five glorious years. The man was utterly broken up. He didn't go to the office next day. He didn't know he *had* an office. Five thousand Armenians—yes, but that little girl was *his very own.* And no one must call him selfish. We all react like that. God made us like that. During the war we all learnt to read the casualty lists casually—until a yellow envelope was thrust into our hands and we learnt that out of the red generality of horror, dimly realized, the bloody hated hand of war had reached out and taken *our* brother, *our* father, *our* sweetheart, *our* son. And, after that, war took on a new horror, and we never read the casualty list again without a kind of ache of sympathy for all those who now were feeling as once we felt. The thing had become personal, and so it had come home to us.

Now, the first thing to say about religion is that it is a personal thing, or it is not religion. We who teach religion—local preachers and class-leaders and Sunday-school teachers—all ought to understand that at the beginning. The test of a sermon, for instance, is not whether it is educative and satisfies a quite worthy intellectual curiosity as to the meaning of a passage. If we call it a sermon we must relentlessly ask ourselves this test question: Is it going to help people to live? Does it actually touch life and come to grips with the things men are daily facing? Does it send them out with new courage and hope to climb the shining way? We must not be satisfied if a man goes away and says, 'That was a fine sermon,' or, 'That was a fine preacher.' We must not be satisfied till people go away and say, at least to themselves, 'That made a difference to *me*'; 'That's going to help *me*'; 'That makes life more meaningful to *me*.' No religion that is divorced from life is going to make an appeal; for, as we have seen, the personal interest is supreme.

The second thing to say is that religion is such a personal thing that we must not treat it as though it were a movement, as, for instance, the R.S.P.C.A. is a 'movement,' for it is not personal on our side only; it is personal on God's also.

Quite a number of people, many of whom cannot diagnose their own disease, have got the notion that Christianity is a kind of movement; a movement worthy of support and doing a great deal of good work, but still a movement. It has to be said that such people are not Christians at all, though a good many of them are in office in churches, and some are in the ministry. You find them going about recommending their religion, as a movement, with some degree of misgiving; and they are surprised when people pick up the misgiving and don't pick up the religion. Some of them are very lovable, very pathetic souls, who don't realize how utterly they have missed the way, and what an enormous lot they are still missing. They do often wonder why their life seems to be without power, why life seems to lack meaning and beauty, why certain secret sins have such deadly dominion over them, why the way is so steep and tortuous, why others pass them with radiant faces and a song on their lips, while to them life is all so grey and drab. I am afraid in many cases it is because they are supporting a movement, a movement which they can see is doing excellent work. Strictly speaking, they do not know what religion is, because religion means a binding back of the soul to God, a definite personal relationship, a link between a man's soul and the heart of a great Father.

I sometimes think that is where Joseph of Arimathea was. He thought Christianity was a movement. It commanded his respect. As a movement he believed in it. Very late indeed—one had almost written too late—did he discover that it is first of all a relation to a person.

He bears Him to His new-wrought tomb,
Jesus, to whom he would not bow.
He leaves Him in its sacred gloom,
His Lord and Saviour, *now*.

There is not enough life and inspiration in belonging to a movement however splendid. We want the personal relationship. We want a heart to turn to, a heart that understands and loves and sympathizes and kindles our devotion. We want some one who binds us to Himself so that, without cant or unreality or humbug, we can say, 'My Beloved's mine, and I am His.' *Then* the new song begins.

Heaven above is softer blue,
Earth around is sweeter green:
Something lives in every hue,
Christless eyes have never seen:

Birds with gladder songs o'erflow,
Flowers with deeper beauties shine,
Since I know as now I know,
I am His and He is mine.

Moreover, a movement always seems to me to lack security. I do not mean financially, though it is a not uninstructive distinction between a movement and a relationship to point out that many very worthy movements would peter out but for financial aid. But even valuable movements have petered out in other ways, sometimes in bloodshed; movements for reform and civilization and liberty, fraternity and equality. Many of these movements have served us, and serve us still, contributing to our comfort and security. I am grateful for them. But I know that there are forces abroad in the world big enough to smash every movement in it, and to smash it utterly. I remember as a young subaltern in Mesopotamia hearing a lecture given by a famous Oxford professor who came to tell us how to deal with Arabs. I have forgotten most of it, but I do remember that he talked about progress in a most optimistic way. He went back to the time when we were monkeys—or, rather, when other people were—and then he showed the progress which made us into cave-men who wore a skin or two and blipped their neighbours over the head in order to steal their wives; and so on till he came to the modern man. He juggled with the magic word 'evolution.' He showed us how the modern man had wireless and telephones and motors. . . . The effect he produced on a party of semi-somnolent officers was that we were all in a kind of lift or escalator. Humanity was progressing up and up and up, willy-nilly. I suppose there is enough truth in it to make people purr with content; but I cannot find anything inevitable about progress. What about Greece and Rome and Babylon? I need not go so far. I look into my own heart and I know that if I get a little bit careless and a very little bit prayerless, I go right down to the very bottom with a bang. And I simply daren't trust any movement. I want a personal relation with God which is big enough and real enough to hold me up if all the ships on the sea go down, and if every 'movement' in modern life breaks up and perishes. And the man whose religion doesn't make him quite sure that he has got that, hasn't got the biggest thing that religion has to offer.

We may all have it for the taking. 'He loved *me*, and gave Himself up for *me*.' I sometimes find myself saying that, Coué fashion, over and over again. A census man was going his rounds, and he knocked at one door to learn who lived behind it. He asked the woman who opened it what children she had. She said, 'Well, there's Willie and 'Orace and Ethel——' He interrupted 'Never mind names, I just want numbers.' Then *she* grew indignant. 'They haven't got numbers; every one of them's got names.' Exactly; because there was a personal relationship between the mother and each of her bairns. 'He calleth them all by *name*.' Some writers in the Old Testament were so anxious to prove the greatness of God that, for the moment they overlooked that relationship.

They referred to the nations as drops in the bottom of a bucket, and—what no congregation would stand to-day—they referred to the inhabitants of the earth as grasshoppers. The Psalms are personal. And Jesus crowns that gospel for the individual: 'Not a bird hops down from a twig to the ground'—as I am told the Aramaic text suggests—'but your heavenly Father is concerned in the happening.' And, in a glorious poetic exaggeration, 'Even the hairs of your head are numbered.' Jesus crowns that gospel not only by word but by deed. Is there anything more lovely in the New Testament than the way in which He will unhurriedly spend time with individuals? His hours were all full, as those of all happy men are. Yet He was never too busy to turn aside and give His ungrudging best to people; and, what is more, those people never guessed how busy He was. One of the most wonderful revelations of the Christian way ever given was given to one man on a roof at midnight. One of the most wonderful revelations of the character of God which the world possesses was given to one woman of doubtful reputation by the side of a well on a sultry afternoon. Even on the cross, in the midst of His agony, He can make a tryst with a dying thief; and the Gospels are full of His 'Thou's' and 'Me's.'

This is not a narrow creed. If it is egotism, it is a higher egotism, for it is an egotism which is the only true basis of altruism. And the quality of the one will determine the strength of the other.

> What *we* have felt and seen,
> With confidence we tell.

Rock of Ages cleft for the world! Yes, there is a time for that sentiment, but you cannot begin there. The world won't believe you unless, with undry eyes and unsteady voice, you are compelled to sing first,

Rock of Ages, cleft for *me.*

Is your life dissatisfying, tangled, un-unified, all out of harmony? Does God seem unreal and far away? Does prayer seem like talking to nothing? Do certain sins seem utterly beyond your power to conquer? Do all the forms of organized religion get you nowhere? Do you find that all the things that fill your life leave it inexpressibly empty? Do you find that with a thousand friends you are as lonely as if you had been thrown up on a desert island where no one came or had come since the making of the world?

What you need is a personal closure with God, who loves you, and wants you more than you have ever wanted Him in the hungriest moments of your life. That is a very old solution of life's difficulties. It is still the only one there is. Life will never be beautiful, never be satisfying, never be radiant, never be meaningful, until you give up feebly supporting a movement; until you give up a half-condescending acquiescence which costs you nothing; until you give up wanting His way on Sunday night, and having your own way from Monday to Saturday; until you give up yielding only languid admiration to the Wearer of the Crown of Thorns; until you give up pretending to be a Christian, and then compromising as though He mattered nothing at all.

God, the greatest Lover of the human soul, leans out of His immensity to say, '*My* child.' He waits for as personal a response, '*My* Lord, *My* God.' Then life will begin all over again for you.

IX

THE FRIEND WHO DRAWS NEAR TO US IN OUR FRIENDS

Hush, I pray you !
What if this friend happen to be—God ?

R. BROWNING :
' Fears and Scruples.'

IX

THE FRIEND WHO DRAWS NEAR TO US IN OUR FRIENDS

THERE is not one of us who, at some time or another, has not felt that God has drawn near to him through Nature. The purity of a dawn, the glory of the sky at sunset, the morning carol of the birds, the murmur of the sea at night, the strength of the hills, the freedom of the moorland, the majesty of the stars, the splendour of the storm—all these things, at some time or another, have made God seem near to us. There has been a hush of the spirit, which some of us feel to be one of the chief signs of the Presence.

Yet must it not be true to say that, if God can get near to us in inanimate things, He must be able to get much nearer to us through our fellows? If He can speak to me in the tones of the wind, cannot He say much more to me in the vibrant tones of my friend's voice? If the sight of a flower can speak to me of tenderness—and I think that is His voice—then, as I look into the eyes of my friend, how much nearer can God come, how much more clearly can He speak? There is certainly a 'silence that is in the starry sky,' a 'sleep that is among the lonely hills'; and these are His; His ways of hushing the spirit. Then how much more can the belief of my friend, his trust in me, his love for me, his peace-breathing friendship, become the channel through which God draws near to me! 'Hush, I pray you! What if this friend happen to be—God?'

The minister's life is full of interest. It must be quite the most fascinating job in the world, given only one qualification, a great love for humanity. Given that, even a doctor's job is a poor second; for the glory of healing bodies comes only second to the sacred wonder of being allowed to minister to souls.

Can you see this little picture of a part of my job? Can you see a darkened room in a hushed house wherein is scarce a voice that is quite steady? In one corner can you see an old white-haired woman sitting in a low chair, her face half hidden by her hand? Her other hand is on the shoulder of a younger woman, little more than a girl, who is sitting at her feet. There is a fire in the grate. It flickers up now and then, fitfully, as if half afraid of asserting itself too merrily in that house of sorrow. Yet, when it does, it lights up the white hair of the one, and the pale gold of the other. The younger had only been married three months, and then death stalked her young, brave husband through pneumonia and brought him down at last. It was the day after the funeral. Suddenly the younger woman turns almost ferociously on me, standing behind them both. 'Where is God?' she demands. 'I've prayed to Him. I've asked Him to come and be near me in my sorrow. Where is He? Away somewhere above the sky, or something! Why doesn't He come near me and make me know He *is* near? You preached once on "The Everlasting Arms." Where are they?' When the tears and storm were over I felt the only thing I could do was this. I drew my finger-tips lightly down the older woman's arm. 'They are here,' I said. 'They are round you even now. These are the arms of God. . . . "Where is He?" you say. "Why doesn't He come near me?" . . . Hush, I pray you! What if this friend happen to be God?'

No one would ever dream of asserting in face of all the experiences of the saints and mystics that God never draws near to man directly. Some of us have ourselves had experiences which we can describe in no other way. But God knows and loves those who have never credited a direct experience, so unpractical is what they call their practical temperament. So the great Father draws near to them in their fellows. The danger is lest we should miss God when He comes to us in our fellows. A man prays for guidance in some perplexity. I want to ask some of my friends what they expect to happen. Do they expect a voice from heaven? Do they expect that, if they rise and open a Bible with a finger all ready, God will guide it to a passage which will answer their prayers? I knew a man who did that, and his finger hit on the passage, 'He shall be tormented with fire and brimstone.' He shut the book. He never tried that dodge again. I knew another man, a splendid Christian, who went to a great city to start business; and when he came out of the station he didn't know which way to go to look for the shop he intended to buy, so he prayed about it and then he determined he would follow the first white horse. That was his way of getting guidance. Don't you think that if he had sat down and thought about the matter, and then consulted his friends, he would have had a far better chance of finding God's will?

A man once said to me, 'I prayed about it and nothing happened; so I took the advice of my friends and decided it by myself.' I wanted to quote, or misquote, Browning to him: 'Hush, I pray you! What if those friends happen to be God?' What else did he expect to happen? God can surely get much nearer to us through our friends than through the tail of a white horse. If a man is in a dark room of experience and suddenly a blinding light shines upon him which he cannot understand or explain, like the uncanny light we see in pictures of St. Paul's conversion, then he thinks it is God, and that God is near him. But if a friend comes into the room and turns on the electric light which he didn't know was there, then he tends to dismiss the thought of the help of God altogether. 'Hush, I pray you! What if that friend happen to be God?'

My brother, has God given you a wife to whom you can turn; who will minister to you without weakening you, who will accept you when you are embittered with all the stress and strain of life, and by love's alchemy turn that bitter into sweet, saving your belief in humanity by her own? Can she hush your fevered spirit? Can she laugh with you? Can she rejoice in your success without making you vain? Can she go down with you into the deep places of failure without making you morbid? Can she receive you when you have made an utter fool of yourself, and, without blinding her eyes and yours to your foolishness, can she help you to 'see life steadily and see it whole'? Can she, if need be, listen to your hot, foolish, resentful words, and wait with quiet eyes, like homes of silent prayer, till the storm is past, and then, without letting you pose as a martyr on the one hand, and without argument on the other hand, can she guide your feet into the way of peace? Then on to your knees, man, every night of your life, in humble gratitude that God is near you, *so* near you. You think you have only a loyal wife and a true friend. 'Hush, I pray you! What if this friend happen to be God?'

It was perfect friendship, after all, which taught men the ineffable mystery of the Incarnation. A little band of men by the grace of God were received into a friendship. Their Friend was tempted just as they were, yet He never fell. Their Friend knew what fear was, yet it never swayed Him from His purposes. Their Friend knew the petty irritations of life, the way life has of thrusting up its cares before the mind; yet before those deep, clear eyes worry slunk away ashamed, seeing in their depths the horrid reflection of itself. Their

Friend was jostled by the crowd, continually besieged, never allowed a moment's peace if the crowd could find Him. They themselves in His place would have been jarred beyond words. Their nerves would have frayed under the strain. They got irritable even on His behalf. 'Send the multitudes away!' was their cry. But 'He was a Refuge for every hunted life.' He had time for every one. He was never too busy. He was never fretted. He was never hysterical. He was always ready to receive men, and listen to them, and show His belief in them; always eager to heal their souls and minds and bodies; always speaking words of authority and pardon, of strength and graciousness.

Time came when their Friend was suspected, was deserted—yes, even by themselves. Time came when He was tried, mocked, scourged . . . crucified. Yet He never stopped loving, and from the depth of His agony breathed a prayer of forgiveness, and made friends with a dying felon on the cross next to His own. Dead? Oh, yes, He was dead—just like other men. No doubt there were plenty of people in Jerusalem who used those four words—'just like other men.' The disciples maybe used them themselves—'just like other men.' But one morning the dawn broke fresh and gloriously. There was the wild story told by a woman. There was a race to a tomb. There was a Presence, here, there, everywhere, and they began to ask one another a question—'Hush, I pray you! What if this Friend happen to be God?'

There is a sense in which every man is an incarnation of God. Divinity is not in a different category of thought from humanity. Divinity does not consist in ability to do wonderful things like making stars or healing paralytics. These achievements may require power, but not necessarily divinity. The meaning of divinity will be understood when we get away from those values to moral values, not *power* to heal a paralytic but pure *desire* to do so; for divinity shines out in love, compassion, lowliness of heart, passion to serve and uplift, to comfort and strengthen; and, to the extent to which a man is good—in the best sense, the most virile sense of that great word—to that extent he manifests in his humanity the very nature of God. In Jesus men saw friendship raised to its highest power, and the truth burst upon them—'This Friend must be God.' 'We beheld His glory,' cries John in rapture, 'glory as of the only Son of a Father,' full, not of magical works or pompous authority, but full of winsomeness and sincerity, 'full of grace and truth.'

Let us try to learn our lesson then. God, whom so many of us think far off, is near us, near us in our fellows. Let us be quicker to recognize His presence. But let us see further how great is the privilege that, if we draw near to men to help them, we are bringing God near to them. . . . 'You preached on the Everlasting Arms,' the woman said, 'where are they?' We must be God's arms, 'to comfort and succour all those who in this transitory life are in trouble, sorrow, need, sickness, or any other adversity'; God's eyes, so quick to see that need; God's ears, so ready to listen to the outpoured, overburdened heart; God's feet, so quick to run His errands; God's fingers, to do His work.

There is a passage in *My Lady of the Chimney Corner* I cannot help quoting:

> 'God takes a han' wherever He can find it and jist diz what He likes wi' it. Sometimes He takes a bishop's and lays it on a child's head in benediction, then He takes the han' of a docther t' relieve pain, th' han' of a mother t' guide her chile, an' sometimes He takes th' han' of an aul craither like me t' give a bit comfort to a neighbour. But they're all han's touch't be His Spirit, an' His Spirit is everywhere lukin' fur han's to use.'

When I lived in Manchester I used sometimes to go into a Roman Catholic church to say my prayers. The Church of the Holy Name was always open; it was near my home; and it is the most beautiful church in Manchester. On one occasion I was present when they were celebrating Mass. The priest uplifted the Host. To those worshipping, it was the real presence of Christ. They believed that God came near to them in a wafer. A little child had wandered out into the aisle. He seemed to be lost. He began to cry bitterly. Then a man next me rose from his place, gathered the little chap in his arms, and sat down. I can hear now his

'There, there!' uttered in tones so tender as to make one think very beautiful things of that man.

Talk of the Everlasting Arms! Why, they were nearly touching me. The man was comforting a little child for God. It would be as true to say that God was comforting a little child through the arms of a man. When I passed out of that beautiful church I knew I had been near to God, yes, nearer than the priest who handled the Host; for if God can come near to man in a wafer, I think He can come even nearer in the love of a big-hearted man. And I prayed that the God who became incarnate once and perfectly in Man might more and more fully become incarnate in all men and women, that our feet might be guided into the way of peace.

X

THE FRIEND WHO DRAWS NEAR IN THOSE WE BEFRIEND

There is Thy footstool and there rest Thy feet where live the poorest, and lowliest, and lost.

When I try to bow to Thee, my obeisance cannot reach down to the depth where Thy feet rest among the poorest, and lowliest, and lost.

Pride can never approach to where Thou walkest in the clothes of the humble among the poorest, and lowliest, and lost.

My heart can never find its way to where Thou keepest company with the companionless among the poorest, the lowliest, and the lost.

RABINDRANATH TAGORE.

X

THE FRIEND WHO DRAWS NEAR IN THOSE WE BEFRIEND

In the last chapter we thought of the Friend as coming near to us in those who help us. His guidance may come to us as their advice. His comfort may come through their handclasp. His rebuke may come through their sorrow; and so on. In this chapter I want us to see that He comes near to us, not only in those who help us, but in those whom we help.

This has almost become a commonplace. The words of Jesus, 'Inasmuch as ye have done it unto one of the least of these My brethren ye have done it unto Me,' have made us familiar with the thought. Yet I believe that, in a truer sense than we dream, to go to men simply in order to help them is to bring oneself into close touch with the Friend. Those who serve my sons serve me, but their lives do not necessarily touch mine; but of him who serves another in Christ's name it may actually be said, his life touches Christ.

Tolstoy has brought this out in his story, *Where Love is, God is.* Martin, an old cobbler, is reading about Christ and half wishes Christ would visit him. He falls asleep musing, and is startled by a voice which says, 'Martin, Martin, look into the street to-morrow! I will come!' The old cobbler cannot make up his mind whether the voice is real or whether it is just a dream. The next day he finds himself continually going to the window: 'Will He indeed come, I wonder? It is too much to expect, and yet such things have happened.' During the day the old man brings in a sweeper from the street, gives him tea, and invites him to warm his hands by the stove. Then he brings in a soldier's wife whom he sees from the window trying to wrap up her baby in a piece of old sacking, and he gives her food and drink and comfort. Then he brings into his little room an apple-woman and the boy who had run away with one of her apples. As he talks to her, her anger disappears, and, when he dismisses them, the boy is helping her to carry her load. The last scene shows Martin sitting at the table on which burns a solitary candle. 'The day is nearly over and He hasn't been. It must have been a dream after all. Yet His voice seemed so real.' But, as the old man sits there, the figure of the snow-sweeper rises up before his eyes, and a voice says, 'Martin, Martin, do not you know me? This is I.' Then the figure of the soldier's wife with the child in her arms appears out of the darkness, and the Voice says, 'And this is I.' Then follows the figure of the apple-woman, and the Voice says, 'And this also is I.' And the great truth dawns upon the old cobbler that God has come near to him in man, that in loving service to men and women he has actually served the Christ.

All this is probably familiar to us as poetry. For many years I thought of it as poetry, or, perhaps one should say, poetic fancy: a beautiful way of expressing the idea that service to man is service to God. The Indians have an interesting thought that it is always a privilege to help a Brahman, even a Brahman beggar, because you are helping a man in whom God dwells more fully than in any other caste. Jesus, it seems to me, would teach, as a similar thought, that it is always a privilege to help anybody, because all men are of the same caste, the very highest caste. They are all sons of God. They are men in whom God dwells. And, indeed, I think it is not poetic fancy merely, but the naked truth. That by coming to men with nothing but a loving desire to help them you do actually come near to God Himself; perhaps nearer than when you kneel before the altar. And if I were asked to prove that point I should say that the proof lies in the fact that you cannot render disinterested service without feeling a nobler and a better man. No one can go and do a kind deed to another without feeling the better for it; and may we not say that, every time you really feel nobler and better, your feeling is an indication that you have drawn near to God? This is a fact that we ought to keep in mind when we pray that we may know God's nearness. Some think dimly of a vision. Some, like old Martin, half expect to hear a voice. To others God's nearness is limited to feelings they have on Sunday nights in church, and a good many splendid people discredit their experiences of God because, as they say, 'I never see anything. I never hear a voice. I never feel particularly uplifted in a service.' But surely part of the answer is that whenever thought has its horizons widened and its object directed from self to another; whenever feeling is not just emotion, but a deep passion for the well-being of others; whenever will is strengthened, not in the direction of success for oneself, but of service for others, then just because thought, feeling, and will, the three parts of the self, have all been enlarged, is not this an absolute proof that God Himself has drawn near to us, though He may have drawn near at such a depth that we cannot distinguish completely between Himself and ourselves?

I have met men and women who have expressed desires to serve, say on the mission field, or in the ministry, or in some other sphere of service, and they have told me that they are only waiting for 'a call.' The question I always want to ask them is this: 'What do you expect to happen?' Do you expect God to come to you in a vision, or in a dream, or to call you by name, or to come near to you in some uncanny way? What if your own desire to serve Him is His Voice? Granted that the desire is freed from self-interest, may that very desire not be a call? For whence has that desire come? It has come from a realization of the need of men, and that itself is a challenge; and the fact that you have seen the need, can scarcely rest because of it, makes it a personal challenge; and, quite reverently, what other way has God of calling you? The need of the world is God's call. Your appreciation of that need is God's call to *you*.

Of course, it will depend on how we serve our fellows whether in that service we actually draw near to God. We may compare in our mind Napoleon and Wilberforce. The former would claim to have served humanity, and particularly France, but what was this service compared with that of Wilberforce, rich in fortune, frail in health, hampered by bitter opponents, fighting as real a battle, waging as real a war as the other? On the day when victory came and the slave trade of the British Empire was finally doomed, Sir Samuel Romilly, amid the cheers of the House of Commons, compared the war which Wilberforce had waged with that which Napoleon had waged. Napoleon in his warfare found himself. Wilberforce found God, and he has told us in stirring words that, in the sorrowful faces of negro slaves, he saw the shadowed face of God. And according as our service to man is cleansed from self-aggrandizement will God be able to draw near to us. Why is it that through his very work Wilberforce becomes a better man, and Napoleon does not, unless it be that, in the former case, God is continually near to His own servant?

A member of our Samaritan League said a thing to me two or three days ago which I am sure he would not mind my repeating. It was one of the most beautiful things I have ever heard a man say in my life. He said, 'When I go out to do a service to another man in the name of Christ I feel I have not had an experience with that other man. I have had an experience with Christ.'

For this reason our service must never be superficial. To give a man at the door a shilling may either be serving both God and man, or it may be blasphemy. One comes to feel that it is immoral to escape from the demands of a situation by getting rid of a person with a shilling. The money we give, and the gifts we give, should not be an escape from the situation, but should represent real interest, real sympathy, real love. A shilling should be a translation of personality into terms of cash. If it be that it is all right. If it be less than that, it robs the situation of its possibilities to bring God near to us.

After all, the only service of God is the service of man through whom He comes near to us. We call the hour of worship 'a service'; but divine service begins when we go back to our work again, and the one can only be a preparation for the other. Although it is true to say God comes near to us in many ways, comes near to us directly—I believe with all my heart that the hush which has so often fallen upon us within the sacred walls of our churches is the real presence of God Himself—yet I believe also that God is just as near to us, and more able to be truly served, when we go out into the world and touch the lives of our fellows. It is one thing to escape from the world, to some extent, and be moved to our very soul by the sense of His presence in a church; it is another thing to go out into the world and feel Him near to us, in those so hungry for love and service.

Hundreds of people are earnestly seeking God.

He will come to you, my reader. He comes to all who seek Him. Indeed, our very seeking is the activity of Himself, seeking us. He has His own secret way to every heart. Many times already He has been very near. When love came to you He came. Do you remember? When you took your little one out of His arms into your own, He was there. You will remember that? When you stood by quietly while He took a life you loved back into His arms, though you so yearned to hold it longer in your own, you remember how close He was then? Oh, there have been thousands of times—in a child's laughter, in a woman's love, in the kindly ministries of nature, in music, in art, in literature, in the bread and wine, in the friends who help you. But, my brother, it may be that He is calling you to find Him nearest in those whom you will go out to love for His sake. 'There is Thy footstool, and there rest Thy feet, where live the poorest, and lowliest, and lost.'

XI

THE LENGTHS TO WHICH THE FRIENDSHIP GOES

Into the woods my Master went,
  Clean forspent, forspent,
Into the woods my Master came,
  Forspent with love and shame;
But the olives were not blind to Him,
  The little grey leaves were kind to Him,
The thorn tree had a mind to Him
  When into the woods He came.

Out of the woods my Master went,
  And He was well content.
Out of the woods my Master came,
  Content with Death and Shame.
And when Death and Shame would woo Him last,
  From under a tree they drew Him last,
And on a tree they slew Him, last,
  When out of the woods He came.

SYDNEY LANIER :
'A Ballad of the Woods
and the Master.'

XI

THE LENGTHS TO WHICH THE FRIENDSHIP GOES

THE trouble about religion, and the reason why it seems so difficult to so many of us, is that not only have we got to try to think our way through certain problems, but we have to unthink the thoughts of our great-grandfathers and those who lived in the old times before them. If one may change the figure, we want some new mental clothes. Not one of the readers of this chapter would be seen in the clothes of his or her grandparents. Yet the clothes in which we dress our thoughts go farther back than that. They are—as Carlyle described them to Tennyson—old Jewish rags. And especially is this true in regard to the death of Christ.

The Jews believed that if they offered a lamb or a goat or a bullock, and carried out certain ceremonial, then in some unexplained way their guilt was transferred to the beast. In a sense, it bore their sins and took them away. When Christ was hounded to death by the hatred of Pharisaic plotters, who trembled for the national religion, doomed to disaster if Jesus were proved right, His followers, Jewish in outlook, evolved the theory that the Crucifixion, while consummating, yet remained in the same category with, the long list of Jewish sacrifices. The sin of all the world, past, present, even future, was heaped upon His head. He bore the sins of the world away. 'Behold, the Lamb of God which taketh away the sin of the world.'

This view of the matter compels one's sympathy. Here were the earliest followers of Christ, mainly Jews, facing the appalling tragedy of the Cross, and trying desperately to understand its meaning. They interpreted it with the mental resources at their disposal. They made it fit in with a Jewish scheme of thought. What else could they do or be expected to do? We are not Jews. Yet have we not taken over this same scheme of thought? The thesis of this chapter is that we ought very reverently to unwrap the Jewish rags, look at the matter with twentieth-century eyes, and make sure that ancient forms of thought are not getting in the way of more helpful, because, to us, more reasonable, methods of approach. We are reasonable beings, and God does not expect us to juggle with our minds.

There has been, of course, progress from the Jewish standpoint, though, unfortunately, the shadow of Jewish thought—and I think it is a shadow—still lies very heavily across all hymn-books. Multitudes of our people have not progressed beyond the mentality of the hymn with the chorus, 'Wash me in the blood of the Lamb,' which one may be forgiven for saying is repulsive sentiment, antiquated theology, frightful poetry, set to a very inferior tune.

Yet, though there has been progress, many still cling to the legal aspect of the Cross. Crudely and briefly, in their view, God is the Judge on the bench—holy, righteous, and just. Humanity is the prisoner in the dock. The prisoner has committed sin in the past and present, and will do so in the future. The only sentence which will satisfy the Divine Justice is endless hell for the whole human race. Christ in His passion takes this punishment upon Himself. Except for His intervention the sentence must have been carried out. Divine Justice must be vindicated. The eternal law of righteousness must be upheld.

Surely to the modern man a thousand questions leap to the mind. Are we being asked to believe that the sins of Abraham and the sins of Judas and the sins I haven't committed yet but am going to commit next week, have in some magical sense been transferred to the innocent head of Christ? Isn't that a harder strain on my mind than the Jew had when he tried to believe in his sin offerings? Is it justice? Does it make it into justice that the Victim is willing, or that the Judge is the Father of the Victim and dwells in Him even more intimately than any human figure can illustrate?

But other questions crowd to the brain. Does He take away in one act upon the cross the sins of all the world? Sin remains and curses the world, and blasts the lives of men and women and children. It cannot mean that. Does it remove my guilt? Does it remove the effect of sin in me? Is it not one of the most awful facts about sin that

I become identified with it? It has passed into the very fibre of my being and made me what I am. Would to God that some one could take it, like a burden from a weary back, and carry it for me! Would to God that it were a debt to be paid for, or a crime with a penalty laid down which some one else could pay! But, even if it were as easy as that, how could He pay in the past a debt which I have not yet fully scored up in God's account? Can blood that flowed two thousand years ago wash that away? Isn't my salvation the problem of changing me, and can that be done by one act, even if performed by Christ, two thousand years ago? Have we been clinging to a Jewish superstition? Have we been juggling with our minds? Is salvation the paying off of a debt in a legal sense to satisfy an eternal law of righteousness? What is this eternal law of righteousness? And would all humanity have gone to hell if Jesus had not died? Do we expect the man-in-the-street to believe God is that kind of person? Couldn't God forgive without that? Jesus forgave men in the days of His flesh without demanding atonement. I forgive my child without atonement. Isn't God like Jesus? Did He really demand this ghastly murder before He could forgive the race He made?

I have wearied the reader with questions. It will be pointed out that millions have come to a reconciliation with God and yet have believed like that. That is true. But it is also true that God can get at a hungry soul through the most muddle-headed argument in the world; but that is no reason why we shouldn't try to think straight. Can we leave law courts and sacrifices for a moment and argue from more human relations, as Jesus did?

Let us turn to some true stories. The first is taken from *The Meaning of the Cross.*[1] A working man in the north of England found that soon after his marriage his wife was drifting into vicious ways and going from bad to worse. He came home one Sunday evening to find, as he had found a dozen times before, that she had gone on a new debauch. He knew in what condition she would return after a nameless life. He made up his mind that he would not part with her who had already parted from him; that he would give himself at least to the *effort* of winning her back to ways of purity and goodness. He would accept no pity. 'Not a word!' he said, 'she is my wife, and I shall love her as long as there is breath in my body.' She did not mend, and died in his house after some years, in a shameful condition, with his hands spread over her in pity and in prayer. Are we to see the meaning of the phrase 'bearing sin' in the lengths to which true friendship goes?

Take the story that was going about during the Armenian atrocities, and which Dr. Fosdick has recently used. A certain Turkish officer took part in the looting and raiding of a certain Armenian home. The aged father and mother and the sons were taken out and shot in cold blood. The daughters were given away to the soldiery. The eldest was a girl of twenty. The officer kept her

[1] Dr. W. R. Maltby.

for himself. Her womanhood was blasted by his lust. By careful scheming she was at last able to escape to a camp where Armenian refugees were protected by the British. In common with many other similar girls, she was given a nursing training to make it possible for her to nurse her own countrymen and women who were sick. She did very well indeed, and at length was moved to a hospital where Turkish prisoners were being nursed. She was put on night duty in the officers' ward. On the first night of her duty she passed down the ward with a shaded lantern in her hand. Then a glint of light from her lantern flashed on a face she recognized. She stopped, rooted to the ground in horror. She lifted the lantern to make assurance doubly sure. Yes, it could be no other! There lay the man who had wrought the ruin of her home, the murder of her loved ones; whose fiendish lust had desecrated the sacred temple of her body. He was dangerously ill. It would have required no violence, but only inattention, to ensure his death that very night. She confessed afterwards how bitter the struggle in her mind had been. But she nursed him back to health again until the doctors marvelled at her care. When that officer recovered the doctor brought the nurse up to his bed and said to the patient, 'But for this girl's devotion you would be dead.' 'I think we have met before,' the officer replied, white to the lips. 'Yes,' she said, 'we have met before.' When the doctor was out of hearing the officer almost hissed the words at her, 'Why didn't you kill me?' And this was her answer: 'Because cruelty cannot be righted by cruelty, nor violence by violence. I am a follower of Him who said "Love your enemies." That is my religion.' The man lay silent for a long time, and then he spoke. 'I never knew there was such a religion,' he said. 'If that is your religion tell me more about it, for I want it.' Night after night for a few moments she would come and tell him of the transforming love of the Friend of Souls. Does her action help us to understand what the bearing of sin means?

'To bear sins means to go where the sinner is, and refuse either to leave him or compromise with him; to love a shameful being and therefore to be pierced by his shame; to devote oneself utterly to his recovery, and follow him with ceaseless ministries, knowing that he cannot be recovered without his consent, and that his consent may be indefinitely withheld.'[1]

Is not that the work which Jesus consummated on the cross? Do we not see Him loving men, not only when they are lovable, but when they do mean things, heartless things, misunderstanding things? They leave Him in unutterable loneliness of spirit. Many of them leave Him altogether. They all do at the end. They pour suffering and agony and loneliness and disappointment upon Him as if they are trying to see how far they can go before His love breaks down. His love is even thrown back in His face with spitting and mocking and cursing and denial and betrayal. But that great

[1] Dr. Maltby: *The Meaning of the Cross.*

royal love remains unbroken to the end. The only words about those who did Him to death which are wrung from those tortured lips are these: 'Father, forgive them, they don't know what they are doing.' So He passes out, not even then to escape, but still to suffer as love always must, to bear the sins of the world. But of one part of His work well may He say, 'It is finished.' For He has revealed in that brief life and death the eternal nature of the loving heart of God. 'He that hath seen Me'—yes, even on the cross—'hath seen the Father.' He had shown them the lengths to which love and friendship go.

We said that one of the most awful facts of sin is that no one can bear it away for us, for it has become part of ourselves. But there is a far more awful fact than that. It is that we can never bear all sin's entail ourselves. It falls upon our loved ones. It falls most heavily on the One who loves us most—God.

It is not what Christ once did that bears my sins away and saves me, even though He be divine. It is the eternal love whose nature is revealed by that deed which Christ wrought on Calvary. If God is like Jesus, then He loves me with a love which follows all my way; which will never let me go; which, as Thompson's 'Hound of Heaven' illustrates, cannot be shaken off, however man in his wickedness tries to be rid of it; which never burgles the human heart, but continually besieges it with all the wooing, winsome ways of love, never tiring, never giving up, till the walls of pride and hate and indifference are down for ever To such a length does the love of this Friend go.

It is a love more compassionate than man's sin is passionate; more vehement than man's determination to taste the pleasures of sin; more unwearied than man's quest of evil. No man, determined to the utmost bent of his will to give the rein to his evil passions, ever shows the constancy to his purpose which God shows in trying to win him back to Himself. This is the length to which this friendship goes. This is God's eternal and holy purpose, until all men, penitent, are broken down by the sheer vastness of Infinite Love; by the superiority of love's violence over that of hate, of patience over hasty rebellion, of winsome humility over stupid pride, of white truth over murky lies, of beauty over beastliness; until men give up fighting and are overtaken by love, and

> the whole round earth is every way
> Bound by gold chains about the feet of God.

XII

THE ENDLESS FRIENDSHIP AND ITS CHALLENGE

All in the April evening,
  April airs were abroad ;
The sheep with their little lambs
  Passed me by on the road.

The sheep with their little lambs
  Passed me by on the road ;
All in the April evening
  I thought on the Lamb of God.

The lambs were weary and crying
  With a weak, human cry.
I thought on the Lamb of God
  Going meekly to die.

Up in the blue, blue mountains,
  Dewy pastures are sweet ;
Rest for the little bodies,
  Rest for the little feet.

But for the Lamb of God
  Up on the hilltop green,
Only a cross of shame,
  Two stark crosses between.

All in the April evening,
  April airs were abroad ;
I saw the sheep with their lambs,
  And thought on the Lamb of God.

KATHARINE TYNAN.

XII

THE ENDLESS FRIENDSHIP AND ITS CHALLENGE

THERE is in Paris a famous picture by Zwiller called 'The First Night Outside Paradise.' Our fabled parents have been driven out of the Garden of Eden, and are preparing to spend the first night in the desert beyond. In the distance can be discerned the figure of the angel with the flaming sword, but the eyes of the exiles are not fixed upon him. They are gazing far above his head, and there, outlined in light, faint, but unmistakable, the artist has painted a cross. In wondering awe their gaze is fastened upon it. In that picture is enshrined a truth of enormous moment. With human sin came divine suffering. There is a 'Lamb that hath been slain from the foundation of the world.'

We speak of the Cross as though it were a tragedy which formed the climax to the plotting of a handful of Jews, or as though it were one historic act by which the sin of the world was in some way expiated. But the Cross means far more than this. The Cross was planted on Good Friday bearing its awful, quivering load, and a few hours afterwards it was taken down ; but a cross was planted in the heart of God when sin first darkened human history. And that cross will never be removed till the last sinning soul is gathered in. The cross of wood is a symbol of a cross eternal.

The idea of a suffering God is only found in Christianity. We do not find it in other religions. Heaven, in every other religion, is a realm where God, or the gods, enjoy in unruffled serenity, and in a bliss unmarred by the pain of earth, whatever pleasures and delights the mind and imagination of man can conceive for them. This idea of a suffering God is so new that a great many Christian people have not yet got hold of it. Heaven, even to them, is still a realm where God is seated on a throne in pomp and power and glory, surrounded by thousands of fawning angels who wait His bidding, and who listen awestruck to the thundering tones in which He utters His eternal decrees.

But His majesty is the quiet dignity of suffering. His power is the power of love. The searching eyes are full of tears. The voice that calls is broken with sobs. Even when I look on the Cross I can repeat to myself those deathless words of Jesus: 'He that hath seen Me hath seen the Father'; not a father living in some remote sphere unmoved by the world's sin and sorrow, but bearing all its pain and grief and sin in His own heart. And even the song of the angels, as long as earth's sin remains, is set in a minor key. The moan of earth's infinite tragedy sobs through it all.

> Never a sign of passion or of pity,
>   Never a wail for weakness or for wrong,
> Has not its archive in the angels' city,
>   Finds not its echo in the endless song.

The conception of a God who suffers is deepened yet further when we reflect that suffering is His reaction to human sin. When we see a deed of violence, our characteristic reaction is to step in and stop it, using force if necessary I remember standing with a group of officers around the body of an Armenian girl who had been foully done to death. Her body was black and blue with the treatment she had received. Her father was standing there with us. Alternately he cursed and sobbed. I shall never forget the wave of passionate indignation which swept over us at the thought of the outrage that had been committed. If the miscreant responsible had appeared at that moment I do not think there was one of us who would not have drawn his revolver and shot him where he stood. If we, impure as we are, could know, let alone bear, the sin of the tiniest hamlet in England, our brain would be sickened, our soul burn with resentment, our action quicken to vengeance.

Yet, with white-hot anger at the sin of all the world which hourly He bears, there is in the heart of God a love for the sinner as tender as a woman's and as wide as the sea. The saints have taught us His way. When Gandhi's followers so far forgot their master's ideals as to give way to the temptation to violence, their leader never rebuked them save by the most terrible rebuke of all. He would arrest the whole movement which meant so much to him. He would turn aside and punish himself with rigorous asceticism. And his method never failed to bring the offenders to penitence. The Cross of Jesus shows us perfectly God's way. The beloved Son is captured, mocked, derided, beaten, hounded to the place of the skull. A crown of thorns is on His brow. Roman nails pierce hands and feet. The cross is raised upright and dropped with a sickening thud into the hole prepared for it. No outburst of divine wrath engulfs men. No awful Voice breaks the silence. Will not God interpose? When Abraham's son was bound to the altar of sacrifice a voice divine forbade the awful deed. But when the Son of God is bound to the high altar of the world there is no voice to break the silence save the sobbing of a Magdalene. Legions of angels have long been waiting to burst through, but they are held back in the strong leash of love. So it must ever be. Men can never be redeemed by a God who, like some divine burglar, enters the human heart by force, interferes with men's free will, and stays the hand which is bent on evil. The world will only be redeemed by a love which suffers and waits till man at last, satiated with sin, shall turn to see what sin is costing God; who, through the long eternal years, treads His own self-chosen *via dolorosa*, and is nailed by sin to His eternal cross.

We believe that the greatest truth about the Cross is that it is the translation into terms of history of an eternal fact. Calvary is its historical setting, but eternity is its compass; A.D. 29 was the time, but in a truer sense the Cross is timeless. For three terrible hours a curtain is drawn back from the eternal heart of God. I remember one night in the Mediterranean we passed quite close to Stromboli, an island volcano which rises sheer out of the sea. It was after dinner and almost dark. Suddenly there was a great burst of flame from the crater at the summit. Huge tongues of flame shot up hundreds of feet into the sky, lighting up the ocean for miles around. Tons of molten rock were thrown up into the air. Through our glasses it was possible to distinguish red-hot boulders racing down the mountain-side, and gradually a stream of lava forced its way almost to the sea. For many hours—when our vessel had slipped westwards towards the last lingering light of sunset which lay upon the horizon, when the bold outline of Stromboli was lost in the gathering shadows of night—that red-hot stream of lava, like some awful, open wound, gashed the darkness. What did it mean? It meant that for a few hours there had been revealed those great fires which had been burning in the mountain's heart since the foundation of the world.

> I sometimes think about the Cross,
> And shut my eyes, and try to see
> The cruel nails and crown of thorns,
> And Jesus, crucified for me.
>
> But even could I see Him die,
> I could but see a little part
> Of that great love, which like a fire,
> Is *always* burning in His heart.

The Cross itself is the greatest event in all history. Our attitude to it can only be that of adoring, wondering awe. But it speaks of something greater still. The friendship of Jesus, which the Cross could not end, speaks of the friendship of the Father, which began with the dawn of human consciousness in the world, and which will never end. Moreover, the friendship of Jesus, as it meets the test of the Cross, shows the nature of the friendship also of God Himself. Here is a love revealed to our wondering eyes which, long before Christ came, was loving and suffering for men in a manner which only Christ could reveal, and which will go on loving and suffering until the last soul is voluntarily brought into harmony with Himself in the final harmony of the ultimate heaven.

What does all this involve for us? Is it merely a piling up of the agony in which we have no share? Does it not challenge us, in Paul's phrase, to enter the fellowship of His sufferings? And what does this mean? In the first place, it ought to mean a new and terrible realization of what sin is to God. It is 'a raised hand, a clenched fist, and a blow in the face of God.' By sin we wound the heart that loves us with a love we cannot measure; a love which will never let us go.

Oh break, oh break, hard heart of mine!
Thy weak self-love and guilty pride,
His Pilate and His Judas are:
Jesus, my Lord, *is* crucified!

But that is only the beginning. To enter the fellowship of His sufferings is to go farther than that. The story is told of St. Francis Assisi that he pondered for so long the Passion of Christ that at last his hands and feet bore strange marks like the scars of nail-wounds. Many devout souls have often meditated and pondered lovingly the Passion of their Lord, but is this kind of ecstasy of aesthetic sorrow the fellowship of the sufferings of Christ?

I think not. To enter truly into the fellowship of Christ's sufferings is to translate emotion into service, to lessen the suffering of God by fighting the sin of men. The method of the monastery is to evade the issue and become morbid in doing so. The challenge to the disciple is to service. It is said that the Americans in a certain regiment drew papers out of a hat to decide who should go to France and serve in the trenches. The men who drew a paper marked with a cross were chosen to go. To see the vision of an Eternal Cross is to draw a cross and choose a life that means meditation certainly, but primarily front-line service. To share with God the heartbreak of the world does not allow the true soldier of the Cross to sit down and weep. It sends him out to find a new joy set before him; for unselfish sorrow does not inhibit the finest and deepest joy either in heaven or on earth. His song is the song of the first robin, who tugged with its tiny beak till it had withdrawn a spike from the crown of thorns which Jesus wore upon the cross, and then went out to sing a new song, though its own breast was stained with blood.

A friend of mine once told me a beautiful allegory. An angel drew near to the throne of grace, and God said, 'What wouldst thou?' And the angel said, 'I would fain be a saviour of men: the cry of their misery and pain and sin has sounded even in heaven. Suffer me to fly down from above and rescue them.' And the host of heaven drew near to listen. And God said—and His voice was very gentle: 'Thou wouldst be a saviour of men, yet is thine eye bright and happy, and thy heart beats with a joy that has never been dimmed, and thy hands are white and clean. Hast thou not beheld My Son?' And the angel kept silence, for he understood not these things. And God said, 'Go for a season and dwell with men, and see what thou shalt see upon the earth.' And the angel departed. Now, long time afterward there stood one before the throne, and his mien was sad, yet from his presence shone a great hope and a great joy. And God said, 'Who art thou?' And he said, 'I am Thine angel whom Thou didst send to dwell awhile with men.' And God said, 'But thine eye is dim with pain, and thy heart is broken, and thy hands are stained with blood.' And the angel answered, 'I have seen sorrow and pain and sin. The sons of men grind one another for wealth, and spill their brother's blood for power, and trample their sisters that they may know pleasure. And when I saw, my eyes were dim; and when I loved, my heart was broken; and when I strove to lift the fallen, my hands were stained with blood.' And God said, 'And hast thou returned that thy wounds may be healed?' And the angel said, 'No, Lord, for man's sake I would cling to my pain. How else could I save him? Bid me return to the place of man's anguish. I cannot raise him save as I stand and suffer at his side.' And there was a movement in heaven, and all the hosts thereof turned and looked, and behold, a Lamb standing as though it had been newly slain. And God turned to the angel and said, 'Go, for now thou too hast learned to be a saviour of men.'

QUESTIONS

Prologue

p. 11. Did Jesus love unlovable people? If so, did He force Himself to love them, or did He find something lovable in them? What would be the attitude of Jesus to some one He did not like?

p. 14. In the dream of the business man Jesus did not *condemn* him. Would it not have been better if Jesus had violently denounced underhand methods? Do you think you could make a man ashamed of evil without condemning him? Reasons.

p. 15. 'People always feel they want to tell Him all their difficulties and get His help.' Why? If He came to your home, what problem would you ask Him about? 'In His very listening there was comfort.' Is there a ministry we can all exercise on these lines?

p. 16. How would you tell a troubled mother to get this 'inward peace'? Be explicit.

p. 18. Jesus needs no credentials except Himself. Discuss this statement.

p. 21. What does 'that which' mean in the sentence, 'The Son of Man came to seek and to save that which was lost'?

Chapter I

p. 27. May not this use of imagination be self-delusion?

p. 30. 'Imagination is to the will what steam is to an engine.' Discuss this statement.

p. 31. Is it any good reciting the Creed, then, or should creeds be abandoned? Or should they be altered every year or so?

p. 32. An intellectual difficulty is irrelevant because Christianity is not intellectual assent primarily, but a way of life. Discuss this.

p. 34. So what of 'The Imitation of Christ'?

Chapter II

p. 39. 'We are so inoculated with Christianity that we cannot catch it badly.' Is this true?
Does this bear on our treatment of little children?
Does familiarity with phrases describing great religious experiences lessen the chances of realizing them?

p. 43. Why did He invite Thomas to touch Him and yet would not allow Mary to do so?

p. 44. Have you ever asked yourself why clothes were found in the tomb and yet the figure in the garden was clothed? What is the significance of the clothes?

p. 45. Friendship will make us like the friend we admire and see much of. Is this true?

p. 46. What do *you* mean by 'being saved'?

Chapter III

p. 51. ' Jesus was a Jew living two thousand years ago, in quite different conditions and facing different problems. How can He be of use to me to-day ? ' How would you answer this ?

p. 56. ' I believe in the resurrection of the body.' Do you ? What do you mean by ' resurrection ' and ' body ' ? If you mean ' I believe in the survival of personality ' ought you not to say so ?

p. 58. ' Jesus is actually present in the Sacrament.' What does this mean to you ?
How would you suggest to a doubter that Jesus can be made real ?

Chapter IV

p. 64. When you pray, ' Speak, Lord, for Thy servant heareth,' what do you expect to happen ?
Cf. Hymn 763 (*M. H. B.*).
When you pray, ' Be with me, O Lord, to-day,' what do you expect to happen ?
Cf. Hymns 717 and 911 (*M. H. B.*).
Is it morbid to ask such questions as those on p. 69 ?
Should we question the motives of others in this way ?
(*For private use.*)
Read Hymn 424 (*M. H. B.*) and then 249.
And take off your armour first.
Make a list of your sins on paper, sins you would have to confess to a priest if you were a Roman Catholic. Then confess them to God and *accept* His pardon.

Chapter V

p. 73. Thousands say, ' The Church has failed,' and make other criticisms of the Church.
How far is this a criticism in good faith or a personal excuse for compromising with Christ ?
If people loved Christ, would they stand outside and criticize or inside and help, and would they *feel* criticisms of the Church more or less ?

p. 74. If we were really anything like Christ, should we have to advertise, and try to fill our churches, and have bazaars (!) , or would life be so radiant and glorious and victorious and infectious that people would flock to find out the secret of our mastery of life ?
Why are so many athletic-minded *he-men* so shy of the Church ? Would they be shy of Jesus ?
Have we funked the call to sacrifice ?
What sacrifices does Jesus ask of us that we refuse ?

p. 76. Make a list of the things that keep people back from following Christ. (Privately make a list of the things that keep *you* back. Are they worth it ?)

p. 78. What is the effect on personality of offering prayers we are not prepared God should answer ?

p. 79. Why do people go to Church? Why do people stay away?
p. 80. (*For private use.*) Are you on the touchline or in the team.

CHAPTER VI

p. 84. 'Perfect humanity is deity under human conditions.' Discuss this.
Was there any quality in Christ that would not be present if again there lived a perfect man?
p. 85. He won our battle; but had He weapons beyond our reach?
p. 87. What does 'Lead us not into temptation' mean?
Is God likely to do so?
Would you lead a child into temptation?
p. 88. You say, 'Don't worry.' 'I can't help worrying,' says Mrs. Smith. How would you help her?
p. 89. What is the difference between fear and being afraid?

CHAPTER VII

p. 95. We become like the friends we make and admire. Is this true?
If a man said to you 'I want to follow Christ; I want this great experience of Him of which the New Testament speaks; how shall I begin?' what would you say?
p. 102. 'I'm trying to be good,' says a man. Can you tell him anything more?
If not, would that message be worth exporting to, say, India, where they knew that before?
What is the gospel (i.e. good news) of Christ?

CHAPTER VIII

'Are you saved?' asked a Salvation Army officer. What does the phrase mean? Is it important?
Is it selfish to be concerned about saving your own soul?
Can you be saved by forgetting you have a soul in unselfish service for others?
p. 108. What is your test of the value of a sermon?
Make up a definition of 'The Church.' Is it completely described as an 'institution undoubtedly doing good work'?
p. 111. Discuss the difference between a movement and a relationship.
p. 114. Analyse 'that Sunday-nightish feeling.' What are its values and dangers?

CHAPTER IX

p. 119. Does Nature lead men to God? Discuss the fact that people who live in the most glorious scenery (e.g. India and Africa) are sometimes cruel and degraded.
What would you say to a man who says 'I find all the religion I want in the fields and woods, so I shan't go to church'?

p. 121. When you pray for guidance, what do you expect to happen?
How is God drawing near to His children through men and women?
(*For private use.*)
Is He drawing near to men and women through you? If not, why not?

CHAPTER X

p. 132. The story of the cobbler. Mr. Practical says, 'Yes, a pleasant fancy.' Do you agree?
p. 134. What do you mean by 'the call of God'?
Is it different to be 'called to be a missionary' than to be 'called to be a surgeon'? Or a teacher, or an undertaker, or a butcher, or a dustman? How?
p. 136. The vexed question of alms: discuss it.
When you bought those laces, was it a service to God?
When you gave that beggar a shilling, did you love him or want to get rid of him?

CHAPTER XI

p. 141. Put in simple words for an untrained mind your 'theory of the Atonement.'
p. 143. Take these questions one by one, and answer them honestly.
p. 144. If you had lived with Jesus, and loved and followed Him, and died before He did, would you have been 'saved'?
What about Abraham?
So is the Cross 'necessary to salvation'?
Is any 'transactional' view of the Cross sound?
If you think so, what is the transaction?
If not, why did Jesus go through an Agony in the Garden while others later went to death with songs on their lips?
p. 145. What do you mean by 'He bore our sins'?
What do you mean by 'He died for me'?

CHAPTER XII

p. 153. If God suffers, what of the happiness of heaven?
p. 155. Examine your reaction to human sin.
Mr. Jones, reading of a guilty criminal condemned to imprisonment, said 'I'm glad they've caught him. Serve him right.' Mrs. Jones said 'I'm sorry for him. I've done worse things than that, but I've not had to suffer.' What do you say? What would Jesus say?
Do you think forgiveness should mean remission of penalty?
(1) On earth? (2) In heaven?
But would the way of Gandhi work? What then?
p. 158. Will all souls be gathered in?
p. 159. What do you mean by 'the fellowship of His sufferings'?